Don't Gamble on Life Improvement...
Until You Shift the Odds!

Second Edition

Kevin E. Eastman

D1265250

Disclaimer: This publication is sold with the understanding that the author is not, and does not engage in rendering psychological, or any other professional medical services. If expert assistance or counseling is needed, the services of a competent medical professional should be sought.

For family, friends, and fraternity:
Who continue to challenge my way of thinking.

"Our deepest fear is not that we are inadequate. Our deepest fear is that we are powerful beyond measure. It is our light, not our darkness that most frightens us. We ask ourselves, *'Who am I to be brilliant, gorgeous, talented, fabulous?'* Actually, who are you *not* to be?"

~Marianne Williamson, 1992

THE LAYOUT

ACKNOWLEDGMENTS

A lot of time, effort, and sacrifice went into this project. I must take a few moments to acknowledge some of the incredible individuals I've had the pleasure of interacting with over the years. Without them, I wouldn't have learned many of the valuable lessons that continue to guide me through my journey in life.

I'd be remiss if I didn't first acknowledge and give thanks to the Heavenly Father. While no one would mistake me for an evangelist, I know there is no *me...* without *Him!* It hasn't been easy waiting patiently for the plan to unfold, but I've held on to the belief that things always work out as, and when they should. Thank you for the past, current, and future blessings!

My beautiful wife: My love, you've been my loudest cheerleader, and harshest external critic – as it should be. I don't know where I'd be if you hadn't come into my life when you did, but I'm grateful you did. When our paths crossed a second time, it was what I needed to know things would be okay. I barely remember life *before* you, and don't want to imagine life *without* you! You are absolutely amazing!

You kept asking why I had my laptop open "all the time," or why I was always "zoning out." Of course, I didn't agree with your assessment, but here's the culmination of the "zoning out" with my laptop open "all the time." Thank you for becoming my queen, my soulmate, and helping me *find* me. I truly love you beyond measure!

My wonderful daughters: In your own unique ways, both of you have inspired me. It isn't always easy to deal with me, but being your dad is one of the greatest honors I've been awarded, and one I proudly wear. I'll continue trying to be a positive example, because I want nothing but success for you. I hope I'm able to provide you with enough tools, so you're able to achieve every one of your dreams. I love you both more than you realize, or even want to admit!

Mom and Dad: You demanded a lot from me, and I'm grateful that you did. You were tough, but fair – everything a hard-headed young man needed. The knowledge I've gained from you is ten times more than I can ever repay. I may not have gotten everything you wanted me to get, when you wanted me to get it, but I *got* it! You corrected me when I got out of line, congratulated me following triumphs, and encouraged me to keep pushing in the face of defeat. I couldn't ask for two better examples to follow. For the pats on my back, as well as the whacks on my behind, I thank you for laying a solid foundation. I love you both!

My immediate and extended family, friends, mentors, and fraternity: There are too many of you to name individually, so I won't even try. I'll simply say thank you for the conversations, debates, feedback, encouragement, and criticism. The information didn't fall on deaf ears. Our exchanges, both the good, and not-so-good have influenced my thinking in ways I couldn't imagine.

Last, but certainly not least, the discouraged person trying to rebound in life: *You* are the true inspiration for this project! I may not know *who* you are, but I've been *where* you are. I know what it's like to feel as though you have the weight of the world on your shoulders. I also know what it's like to have supportive people in your corner encouraging you through those rough spots. I've poured my heart and soul into this project because I wanted to do what I could to help ensure you are satisfied with the person you see each time you look in the mirror.

The journey to success and happiness is going to be filled with roadblocks, detours, bumps, twists, turns, and potholes. It isn't an easy fight by any means, but it is a *winnable* one! It's important to remember that the journey is put into place so you'll appreciate the destination when you arrive. Perhaps one of the lessons I've learned on *my* rough journey will alleviate some of the roadblocks for you, on yours. Who knows? I may be able to return the favor and provide *you* with some inspiration!

1. "Why Should I Pay Attention to This Guy?"

"Thank you" is the only sentiment that begins to express my appreciation for you opening this book. With literally *thousands* of choices for reading material available, I'm grateful that this time, you chose mine. It makes no difference whether you bought the book, borrowed it, found it, or had it gifted to you. I'm overjoyed you're taking time to read the thoughts of a man from Oakland, California who believes he has beneficial information to share.

Why I chose writing a book as my sharing method is simple. This book is written for the person who feels like their dreams of success and happiness have been dashed, because of the obstacles they're encountering. It's also written for the people who have influence in those people's lives. I've been in both positions. I've personally failed, as well as seen people fail in ways they shouldn't be failing, and believe some of the lessons I've learned can remedy that. Too often, the person doesn't see the forest because they're blinded by the trees, and from my vantage point, there hasn't been a lot of "common sense" assistance available… until *now!*

Several motivating factors contributed to this book, and a number of them will be discussed in the coming pages. However, in my opinion, none of these factors is more powerful than the feeling of overcoming an obstacle. What you're about to read is my journey to life transformation – a combination of my interpretation of a number of obstacles I've faced, and many of the powerful, often uncomfortable lessons I've had to learn to overcome these obstacles.

To get the intended effect of this book, I suggest clearing your mind of what you believe, or have been taught, and simply reading it. It can be easy to pigeon-hole a book designed to assist with improving your life, and approach it with a closed or defensive mindset. Been there, done that, and it's exactly why this book is written the way it is.

First, a word of caution: *Buckle your seat belt, because you are in for a wild ride!* I'm about to challenge your way of thinking on a variety of topics, using some very *unconventional* methods! If you have what is considered "thin skin," it may be a good idea to keep a helmet and some armor nearby. Your world is about to be upended, and your emotions put through the wringer! I know, because my emotions were put through the wringer while I was writing it. Joy, sadness, anger, and surprise – they're all in here, and then some.

At the beginning of almost every non-fiction book, the author strives to establish themselves as a competent authority, aiming to create a bond of trust with the reader, and get them excited about reading the rest of the book. I'll continue that practice, with some great advice I received: *"You never know from whom, or where inspiration will come from."*

I'm certain a degree of skepticism arises when you're introduced to a book written by a first-time, relatively unknown author. It doesn't help matters when the author makes a claim like, *"This book can assist you with improving your life."* Don't worry if you're skeptical, at the moment. I'd be skeptical as well, and take no offense with anyone who may be. In fact, two questions probably come to mind: *"Who is this guy?"* and *"Why should I pay attention to him?"*

Both questions are valid, and my answer to the first one will be displayed throughout the book. *"Who is this guy?"* Well, I've experienced the overwhelming majority of the obstacles you're going to read in this book. I've encountered, and found effective ways to overcome them. The chapter titles did *not* come about, by accident! They were selected to chronicle the transformation of a person from *"was"* to *"am."*

Who *was* I? I *was* "that" person. I was that person who needed to find out who I was. I was that person who stayed within my comfort zone, because a fear of winning. I was that person who viewed the glass as half-empty, instead of half-full. That person who dealt with hate, and endured multiple failed relationships? That was me, too! I was also that person who'd fallen victim to peer pressure too many times to count. For a long time, I had the deep longing for validation. So, life experience has taught me a thing or two about how to get over obstacles. It forced me to become who I *am*.

My answer to the second question, however, may shock some folks: *"You don't!"* There's no law that says you have to pay attention to anything I've written in this book. You have complete freedom to choose who you pay attention to, and who you ignore. With that said, I believe you should consider paying attention to what I've written, for a few reasons.

I spent more than 20 years in the U.S. Air Force. The majority of my career was in two particular positions where interpersonal communication was a necessity: drill instructor, and recruiter at the high school, college, and post-graduate levels. In doing these jobs, as well as in my personal life, I've interacted with, and observed *thousands* of people, worn many different hats, and assumed a variety of roles.

Like many people, my life has been, and continues to be full of peaks and valleys. I've been beaten up, beaten down, and at times, completely *broken!* It's an ongoing battle. At my lowest point, life had beaten me so badly, I felt like I was nothing. My self-esteem was in the gutter, depression, failed relationships, dismal finances, etc. I was convinced the world had turned against me, and I was my only line of defense.

Thankfully, in addition to those horrible beat-downs, I received a surplus of helpful information from some great sources. From that, and learning how to get out of my own way, I was able to uncover a number of methods that have helped me decode many of life's most challenging situations. The intent of this book is to explain a few, so you can use them, if you are like I was – tired of the direction your life has been going. Through a lot of adversity I've learned, *"A hand up is better than a handout,"* and the effects *last* longer!

It is imperative that I point out, and you understand, I'm an *extremely* calculated thinker. There's *always* a method to my madness. I'm simplistic in my thought process – logical and methodical in my approach to resolving issues. In my mind, there is no value in unnecessarily complicating things.

Additionally, I don't want to give the impression that the book was written with the intent of talking down to, insulting, ridiculing, or being condescending to anyone. I don't appreciate anyone doing that to me, and I certainly don't want to do that to anyone.

When a person begins reading a book designed for "improvement," there's a tendency to look for scientific explanations of the content. While I have no problems with science, and need to make that clear, in many cases (at least from my experience), plain-old common sense is as, if not *more* effective, and from a common sense perspective is how I've written this book. The idea is to get you into the habit of looking for simplicity in situations. Why? The simpler things are made to appear, the easier they are to understand.

A person may genuinely want to improve, but for whatever reason, will approach a book like this with their guard up. It's usually not done maliciously. It's instinct. Protecting one's self is human nature, but protection with extremism can be a potentially damaging behavioral pattern that needs to be broken, if the person *does* want to improve.

I stated a couple of pages ago that you'd be reading a lot of personal experiences. I decided to take this approach because I want to illustrate how the topics I've included can overwhelm you if you allow them to, and can do it, very quickly. Using my first-hand experience as examples will show you a person who has faced, and overcome a lot of adversity. Displaying my own vulnerability should also minimize, or possibly eliminate many of the biases and defenses an apprehensive reader may not realize are there.

A basic fundamental in communicating effectively is relatability. Communicators need to be able to reach people on common ground, and take it from there. I believe I can relate to most people, thanks to being afforded the privilege of growing up in the so-called "hood," serving in the Air Force, and attending college. These experiences have allowed me to meet, and interact with people from all walks of life, ethnicities, orientations, economic, and social statuses.

I've learned if you carry yourself with confidence and act like you have some sense, your appearance, education, social, or economic status won't be much of a factor. Your communication skills will make the difference. I have no problem conversing with *anybody*, about any *subject*, at any time. I am as comfortable talking with a homeless person as I am with a company CEO, and I have successfully done both.

I'll begin with a rhetorical, yet thought-provoking question: If you're not satisfied with some aspect of your life, and someone told you they might be able to help you turn it 180 degrees from where it currently is, wouldn't you owe it to yourself to at least listen to what they have to say? If you'd listen, you're on the track I want you to be on. If you listened, but ultimately didn't follow their suggestions, the only thing lost (albeit valuable) is time. But, what if the information they provide makes things start making sense? Would you still consider that time lost? Of course not, and that's my point! You have everything to gain if the information helps you.

Maybe *these* reasons are enough for you to consider paying attention to at least *some* of the things written in this book.

Conversely, if you aren't satisfied with your life, but say you *wouldn't* listen... *why not?!* What's the alternative? Stay where you're *not* satisfied? Here's some tough truth, and good luck trying to choke this down: *"If you're not currently satisfied with your life, your plan thus far... hasn't worked!"* Therefore, any alternatives to *your* plan should at least be entertained. You can decide later if the alternatives are stupid or not. *"When the possible ain't working, you must take a shot at the impossible!"* Only then, can you truly say you've tried everything!

Before we get too far along, I want to ensure a few things are clear. This way, you have a thorough understanding of what to expect, and you can't say you weren't warned. You're about to embark on a journey unlike any you've been on. You're headed inside my head (Lord help you!), where you'll be exposed to my ideas, theories, and opinions on a variety of topics I believe contribute most to the chaos we encounter in our lives. You'll agree with some of my ideas, disagree with others. Some of them may sound strange if you've never experienced what I'm describing, but each one has been included with the intent of depicting fairly common situations, from my sometimes very *uncommon* perspective.

This book isn't one size fits all, but it was written with a specific purpose. I'm not crazy enough to believe every topic will apply to every reader. With books like this, there's a tendency with readers, to skip to a topic that interests them, or, as they read, they'll feel the information doesn't apply.

The chapters are *not* intended to be stand-alone, but building blocks from one to the next. I urge you to read this book at least once from beginning to end, without skipping around. Otherwise, you may skip some information you actually *need!*

If you opened this book with the expectation of it being the "stereotypical" self-development book, filled with a bunch of scientific theories, or terminology that belongs in an Ivy League University lecture hall, I have some bad news: *"This ain't that book!"* You won't find any $500 words in here, and it's by design. Even the best information is useless, if the person on the receiving end doesn't understand it. So, I made the effort to ensure what I've written is easily understandable.

Whether you *agree* with the information or not is a different story. You'll be reading a lot of content in this book, and I'm intelligent enough to realize, getting every reader to agree with everything is impossible. I have no doubt, you'll wholeheartedly disagree with some of the things I say, and that's okay. However, I have a much more reasonable goal in mind: getting each reader to agree with at least *one* thing. As the old adage says, *"Rome wasn't built in a day."*

You should prepare yourself, because some of the book's chapters and descriptions are quite lengthy. I hope you weren't expecting a book chocked full of CliffsNotes®. I promise I'm not trying to lull you to sleep, with long sections and descriptions. I just *despise* being misinterpreted. Having to go back and clarify something I felt was initially clear has taught me how profound effective communication really is.

I won't be doing you any favors, if you're an impatient reader. *Despite* our society's inherent desire for instant gratification, or to *"get to the point,"* many of life's most valuable lessons can't be summed up with one-liners. Speed doesn't always translate to effectiveness.

With each topic discussed, I'll be providing facts, logic, reason, and rationale to support my ideas. This should minimize the chance of misinterpretation, and maximize the idea's effectiveness. I chose this methodology, because one of the harshest, yet unforgettable lessons my parents ever taught me was: *"It's impossible to argue with facts without looking <u>stupid</u>."*

You may have already noticed, but many words, phrases, and ideas will be emphasized through the use of exclamations, italics, underlining, and repeating. This is also by design. I may not be physically reading the book for you, where you can hear the voice inflections. Therefore, I must rely on other methods of getting messages across effectively.

At first glance, the repeated things will look like a mistake, but I assure you, it was *intentional.* This is because I wholeheartedly believe in the law of repetition. The more you see or hear something, the greater chance you'll remember it. The more you practice something, the better you *should* become at it. That's how our brains work.

Much of the content in this book is example-based, so it may be tempting at times to wonder, *"Is he talking about me?"* I'll put your mind at ease, right away – I'm not! What you'll be reading is a fusion of many lives (including mine), but none... I repeat *none* of it is intended as a personal attack on anybody, in any way. I don't operate that way, so you can *relax*. Besides, the *only* reason that question would be asked, is you have an idea you may be *guilty* of what's being discussed!

"Nothing is offensive, until it hits a nerve." Words, symbols, and gestures are harmless, until a conscience assigns *meaning* to them. The last thing I ever want to be is offensive, but there is a lot of information crammed into this book, and *"it ain't all nice!"* The topics aren't sugar-coated, and there may be times when the information in a chapter punches you in the mouth, real hard. Sadly, getting punched in the mouth real hard is the only way some people start paying attention.

Nerves will be hit – I guarantee it! However, one thing that will *not* be said at the end of this book is, *"He's lying!"* I'm confident in saying that, because you'll either know, or have seen someone who fits every description I've included. If you can't think of anyone who fits a particular description, it's probably because *you* fit it! I was taught to never apologize for telling the truth, and I'm not about to *start*.

A certain tone is necessary in order for this book to be effective. Therefore, getting through this first chapter will be one of the toughest challenges for some readers. My challenge to *every* reader is if you come across something that gets you riled up, keep reading! I'm well aware that you won't agree with everything I say, but I hope my explanation of those things puts them into at least a *reasonable* context, and quells any initial anger. In case this doesn't happen, the thing to remember is my intent is to get your mind moving, and assist you with progression – *not* to ruffle your feathers.

The idea of improvement can be frightening for many people, due to what may be prompting the *need* to improve. A person may uncover things about themselves they were unaware of, or be forced to acknowledge things they've chosen to ignore, with the latter being the worst of the two.

People become uneasy, possibly overwhelmed, once they realize what's required of them to correct a newly-discovered deficiency. I've been in *that* position, before. One of the lowest feelings I've experienced was having to listen to someone tell me about myself, then, having to look in the mirror and begrudgingly *admit* they were spot-on!

Being forced to eat that big ol' slice of humble pie worked wonders for me. So a person getting angry may not be a bad thing. I say that, because an angry person takes action, and action is an essential element to achieving success. You'll never reach a goal by standing in one spot, talking about how good things would be, *"if only..."* It requires action. You can't begin the process of improving, if you're unable, or remain *unwilling* to admit a problem exists.

"Improvement always starts with an idea, but is advanced or defeated by an attitude." This book will provide plenty of ideas. What you'll have to do is provide the decision to whether you want to use any of these ideas, to create and execute a plan to make adjustments to your life (the attitude).

Some extremely ugly truths need to be, and *will be* exposed. Many of them may be tough to read, especially if you unexpectedly discover that you're the culprit of one of them. However, I feel it's important that they be uncovered, no matter how ugly they are, because denial has never made an issue disappear... *ever!* The issue only festers, and with continued ignoring, can boil over. Then, you'll be trying to resolve the issue using extreme actions fueled by panic, which isn't, nor has ever *been* an effective combination.

You also need to be aware that there are a handful of "colorful" words sprinkled here and there throughout the book. I'm mentioning it now, so you aren't shocked when you come across them. I limited them as much as possible, because using them excessively would undermine the messages, but they *are* there. I included them because for some people, the colorful word will be the thing that makes a message or idea stick. Call me crazy, but I believe the *message* is more important than the *method of delivery*.

I want to make sure another thought is firmly planted in your head: *nothing* I've written in this book should be viewed as a substitute for *professional medical assistance*. This isn't a medical journal, and isn't intended to be. I'll be providing *practical* alternatives, which should help most people, but if something doesn't feel right, and you don't feel you can fix it yourself, seek out the assistance of a licensed professional... period! That's why they exist, and they're good at their job.

At the same time, I don't believe you should go running to a medical professional every time you feel you can't handle a situation. Taking nothing away from professional medical assistance, because quite frankly, some people need it, but in my opinion, many issues can be resolved, and dare I say *prevented*, if you looked within yourself, first. The information

I'm providing to you in this book may save you a lot of time, and possibly save you some embarrassment. It certainly beats paying someone *your* money, to lie on their couch and have them listen to you talk about your feelings.

If you're satisfied with your life the way it is, it's possible that you may feel reading beyond this chapter will be of little benefit to you. I beg to differ! Why? Life may be great as it is, but I don't think many people would argue that it can always be better. Furthermore, you may indeed be satisfied with your life, but I will guarantee, someone you know is *not* as satisfied with *their* life as you are with yours!

So, if you *are* satisfied with your life, there's nothing wrong with paying it forward. Gift this book to someone you believe *would* benefit from it, and encourage them to read it. You may be able to open a dialogue that helps them get back on track. However, my preference is for *you* to read it, first — just in case *my* definition of "satisfied" differs from yours.

On the other hand, if you feel like I felt at one point, like your life is an endless cycle of disappointments and missteps, you have the right book in your hands. I do suggest approaching the topics with an open mind. You must also be willing to adjust your thinking if you discover it's flawed, because you may uncover an obstacle blocking your path to success and happiness that *shocks the hell out of you!*

As I stated earlier, improvement can be painful, due to what you may find is necessary in order to achieve it. This is because what may be necessary is making a decision, or taking an action you don't necessarily *like* doing, or even *want* to do, but unless you *do* it, the situation isn't going to change! One of my absolute favorite sayings goes, *"Change nothing... and nothing changes."*

Should you pay attention to me? I sincerely hope you do. I've provided you with a few reasons why I think you should, but it's a decision you'll have to make. I mentioned earlier that I've experienced and overcome the majority of the obstacles you'll be reading about. So, I'm *well-versed* in dealing with them. If my information and experience helps you overcome even one of the obstacles you've been facing, it's a win-win, but you must remember this: if you decide to take the ride, strap in, because it's going to get bumpy at times. You may discover you're not the person you *think* you are!

You'll need to get comfortable with the possibility of being made *un*comfortable, because some of the things you read in this book might make you feel that way. That isn't necessarily a bad thing. The book may lead you to some uncomfortable places you weren't intending to go, but personal growth is a wonderful by-product of discomfort. There's also the possibility that my suggestions will sound unfamiliar to you, or conflict with your sense of normalcy. The anticipation of this can be unnerving for some people, and for them, the risk will seem high. However, the reward on the *flip side* of the risk is an improved life!

If the possibility of the reward is intriguing to you, layer on some thick skin, put on your big boy (or big girl) pants, strap in tight, and try to hang on! I wonder if *that* was enough to convince you to keep reading?!

2. Finding You, and Why Things Are the Way They Are

Well, *that's* a relief! You decided to continue reading. I can't tell you how encouraging that is. It means: 1) the first chapter didn't bore you to death, 2) there's a chance you see potential value in the coming pages, and 3) you didn't flip out when you read what you should be prepared for. Your curiosity was piqued enough to make you wonder how I'm going to frame the included topics. Initial objective: *complete.*

Alright, the preliminaries are complete. It's time to get to work on a plan for an improved you. The first thing I want to tackle is the meaning behind the book's title. You may be wondering what are the "odds" I'm talking about, how they can be unfavorable, and why would you want to shift them?

The title is of course, a metaphor. I chose it to illustrate a philosophy I believe in, and employ in my own life: *Life unfolds the way it does, as a result of the decisions you make.* The philosophy will become clearer as you progress through the book, and read my recounts of many of the decisions I've made, which haven't always turned out well.

A paraphrased quote often attributed to physicist Albert Einstein states, *"We can't solve a problem with the same thinking used to create it."* If something you've tried has gone wrong in the past, and you want to try it again, but want a different result, a shift must take place in order to achieve the different result. This is where your mindset (the odds) comes in.

Shifting your mindset can completely change a situation's outcome. Hence, the metaphoric phrase, *"shift the odds."*

I've discovered that one of the best ways to right a ship headed in the wrong direction, is through gaining a thorough understanding of whom, and where you are. This provides you with a starting point, or foundation to build from.

Here's the challenge: obtaining this understanding requires *emphatic* self-honesty. For many people, this isn't the easiest task. For them, telling whopping lies when things aren't going right is the preferred method of operation. The lies sound, and make them feel better, so they keep telling them. I've heard people say: *"Sometimes, it's easier to live the lie."* Don't be fooled by this for a second – it's nonsense!

The most dangerous lie you can tell is a lie to yourself. That lie goes from dangerous to destructive, when you *believe* it! If you can't be honest with yourself, you're creating an unnecessary obstacle at the *beginning* of a possible turnaround, and risk impeding your own progress! Let that marinate.

One of the most notorious lies I've heard used when things don't go right is, *"I don't care."* This is such a juvenile response! I almost have to laugh every time I hear someone using it. How do you *not* care if things don't go right for you? Ideally, you don't want things to go *wrong*. So, regardless of what you try to convince yourself... yes, you *do* care!

While you're digesting that, here's another one: *Where you are is exactly where you're supposed to be.* I'd make a note of this, because you'll see it, again. When you do, you should have a better understanding, but it'll require the open mind I mentioned earlier. Sadly, many people have something called an "ego" that interferes with them *having* the open mind. Perhaps the information in this book can chop some of those larger egos down to a manageable (and healthy) size.

As a whole, society needs a behavioral upgrade. Several critical interactive aspects have been damaged, and conflicts have often been the result. Many of the conflicts can be attributed to a miscommunication or misinterpretation. For example, a person reacts to something they've heard. The problem is... what they heard is not what they *thought* they heard, because what they thought they heard is not what was *said!* Read that again, if you need to.

Open communication, and some possibly unsettling conversations are the things needed to resolve the issues. Judging by the way many situations have unfolded, people aren't too keen on having these conversations with *each other* to resolve them. They'd rather avoid or ignore them, and hope they resolve themselves. The problem is this rarely, if ever happens. If having these conversations with another person makes you uncomfortable, try having them with yourself. You can at least build confidence, by talking with someone you're familiar with.

For communication to happen between people, it must first happen within each person. Contrary to many opinions, change *does* occur one person at a time, but before outward change can occur, the person's mindset must be transformed. This poses another challenge, because along with ego, are powerful ideals that have been in your head a while. Your upbringing, morals, and beliefs are all part of your makeup. They significantly impact your self-view, and can generate some major obstacles you'll need to conquer.

I'm not implying that these things be disregarded. You are 100% right to have, and stick to your beliefs… until you try to *force* those beliefs on another person, and *condemn* them if they don't freely accept *your* beliefs! If this occurs, what you've become is judgmental… which is 100% *wrong!*

Who says what *you* believe is correct? More importantly, why would you insist on intruding on another person's freedom to think for themselves? Has it ever occurred to you that *you* could have it wrong? It isn't that far-fetched, contrary to what you've led yourself to believe.

This is why I've repeatedly suggested approaching these topics with an open mind. You may find out that an idea or belief you've held onto is actually flawed. If so, you'll be faced with a dilemma. The more inflexible you are with your beliefs, the narrower your mindset is. Depending on *how* narrow, the already difficult task of improving becomes *more* difficult.

When I was conducting my research for this book, I was stunned to learn just how intertwined these success-depriving subjects really are. Sometimes, they're connected so seamlessly, people don't notice the intersection. I hope your mind is blown as much as mine was, when you discover how many hindrances may be hampering your success and happiness, while functioning and *misleading* you, under the guise of appearing as "a few."

You certainly don't have to, but it may help if you jot down some notes as you're reading. The notes will save you from searching through the entire book to find something you want to recall. Here's a suggestion to get you started.

Write the word *balance* on a sheet of paper. You need to become acquainted with this word, because it's a vital part of the journey to success and happiness. I discuss it in-depth in a later chapter, but for now, you only need an introduction. You'll read about its relevance later, and it'll make a world of difference if my explanation of it makes sense.

The topics I've included are to show how they will create an imbalance if a person isn't careful. This imbalance is what creates many of the obstacles we face. As you continue reading, you'll see how I unwittingly created an imbalance in my life, and the uphill battle I endured to correct my blunder.

If each person makes necessary *individual* adjustments, society would collectively be affected, and naturally get better without us constantly trying to force square pegs into round holes. For this to occur, you must determine if an aspect of your life needs an adjustment, because you may not know it does. This requires uncovering the person you truly are.

What are your likes and dislikes? What makes you behave the way you do? Why do you react the way you do in certain situations? Why do some things bother you a lot, and other things not bother you, at all? Would you be able to recognize if your plan wasn't working, and it's time to change it? Are you *willing* to do what's necessary to change it? These are rhetorical questions, but you need answers to them.

One of the most poignant lessons I've learned is: *a person's reputation or legacy (how they're viewed or remembered) isn't defined by their actions. It's defined by their actions that make the biggest impact on the people they've interacted with.* The impact may be positive or negative, but it isn't controlled by the person performing the action. It's controlled by the perception of the person on the *receiving* end of the action.

When a label is attached to your behavior, the scales get tipped, and everything is off-balance. This may not be to your advantage. Historian Will Durant said, *"We are what we repeatedly do."* Putting this into context, if you're a loud-mouthed jerk the majority of the time, *how* and *why* would someone see you as anything *other* than a loud-mouthed jerk?!

Of course this is all for naught, if you don't *mind* being known as a loud-mouthed jerk. My guess is most people wouldn't feel comfortable being perceived in that manner, if emphatic self-honesty is in place. Therefore, if being branded as a loud-mouthed jerk (which is an extreme) makes you uneasy, the behavior exhibited to counter the branding must be just as extreme. Balance is the key. Just so you know... there are *many* more references to balance following this one.

I mentioned perception, because everyone's perception is unique. This means a single occurrence witnessed by several people can have a variety of effects. It will depend on how the person processes the occurrence in their head.

Under the umbrella of uniqueness is a variety of reasons situations spur their respective reactions. Your character traits govern your perception. Once you understand how they work, you should begin not only to see who and where you are, but why things that have gone wrong, *have* gone wrong.

As far back as I can remember, I've been willing to go "against the grain." I prefer marching to the beat of my own drum, and refuse to allow a person's prejudices, perception, stereotypes, or even popular opinion define who I am, or dictate my behavior. If a person has a problem with me... *they* have the problem! I don't have a problem with me. I've had no choice but to accept who I am, and for that reason alone, I've learned to perform actions that make *me* comfortable.

For example, many people lean to Mickey or Minnie Mouse as their favorite Disney character. I prefer Goofy. Most times, I'll eat my vegetables *before* diving into my steak and potatoes, and my French fries *before* my hamburger. This method of thinking has helped me push through a number of barriers to get where I am. I refuse to let adversity, or widely-accepted practices deter me from something I want, but I didn't always have this philosophy. It took a lot of work.

Now, while I'm on my journey, I want to assist as many people as I can with making sense of the chaos that may be wreaking havoc on their lives. I know first-hand what living this way feels like, and will be the first to tell you, it's not a good place to reside. The only person who can tell you what it feels like to get back up is somebody who's been knocked down, and I'll admit... life knocked me down *many* times!

Figuring out if your life needs an adjustment is a tall order. It'll depend on if you've developed two traits: *diversity* and *flexibility*. You need the ability to adapt to a situation, and come out better than you were before you encountered it. You must learn to overcome obstacles without letting them consume you into oblivion. In the Air Force, I had to adapt my behavior and actions to many situations I found myself in. Why? The mission needed to be accomplished, regardless of the size, difficulty, or number of obstacles in the way.

For this book, I'm defining diversity as the ability to extract knowledge and experience from a variety of sources. This is an important skill to have, because you're exposed to a lot more than you realize. For example, if you've only learned one way to accomplish a task, your scope is extremely limited. You may know *how* to accomplish the task, but may *not* how to accomplish the task *efficiently*. There are times when there is only one correct way of completing a task, but there may be several methods of completing the task that "correct" way.

Flexibility means being able to go with the flow. You're prepared for the unexpected, but you don't have a meltdown if things don't go as you planned. For the tightly-wound person who hasn't learned how to relax, this is difficult to do. Perhaps the way they were raised, or some traumatic life event has made them the way they are, but the impulses to instantly react in a situation must be effectively controlled.

Obstacles will be encountered on the journey to success and happiness. You may as well accept them as part of the process. The best thing for you in combatting them is preparedness. Unexpected obstacles should be respected, but not feared. They can be overcome as easily as the obstacles you can see coming.

I've had the fortune of interacting with many different types of people – everyone from the stuffed-shirted conservative who doesn't say much, to the free-spirited, obnoxious loudmouth who says *too* much. A trait I've been blessed with (or cursed with, depending on your outlook) is the ability to observe a lot and process it, quickly. It doesn't take me long to draw a conclusion, and decide on a course of action. I don't like agonizing over decisions.

However, my experience doesn't lead me to believe I'm better than *anyone*. I do *not* consider myself "superior." I never have, and never *will* accept that adjective about myself. "Superior" people usually don't communicate well with others, and I enjoy talking to, and interacting with people. So being categorized as superior doesn't work for me. At times, I've been told I talk *too* much (which I emphatically dispute), but I wouldn't be the person I am, if I were any other way.

Speaking of superior, there is a select group of people who actually believe they *are*. I'm referring to arrogant people, who think no one is on their level. In my opinion, they miss out on knowing some incredible people, because of their attitude. I almost feel sorry for them… *almost!*

I've come to a realization that arrogant people choose to live in a world created entirely in their head. I'd make a note of the *"in their head"* concept as well, because you'll see it again, once or twice. Well… you'll see it *way* more than that!

To me, arrogance is nothing more than smoke and mirrors. It's a mask for insecurity. In fact, I believe the more arrogant a person is, the more *insecure* they probably are.

From my observation, there are several characteristics displayed by the majority of, if not *all* arrogant people. Most notably, they'll usually do more talking than listening; they're normally louder talkers, too. They'll crudely talk over people, in an attempt to keep the focus on their preferred topic. Lastly, arrogant people love talking about themselves. Why wouldn't they? It's the one topic they believe they know best. I wonder if in fact, they *do* know themselves best?! The content contained in *this* book may provide them with a different perspective on that theory.

Generally, these characteristics are displayed because the arrogant person doesn't want other people to have an opportunity to challenge, or question their way of thinking. Well, why not? They may be forced to realize they're not as good as they thought they were, or even worse... their way of thinking may be flawed. Arrogant people normally don't handle being proven wrong very well, so drastic preventative measures are taken on their part to combat this.

In efforts to stay on their preferred course, they build figurative walls around themselves and assemble their inner circle with people who don't, or refuse to challenge them. This protects the ego, which is extremely fragile in most arrogant people. They're comfortable living this way because it feels safe. Metaphorically, it's a self-imposed exile. The issue is they don't realize they're doing it – or maybe they do.

Here's a statement very few people will argue with: *"If it looks, walks, and sounds like a duck, you can call it a chicken until you are blue in the face... it's a damned duck!"* What's worse is the more you continue to try to *call* it a chicken, the *dumber* you're going to sound to those who know it's a duck! Arrogant people tend to think that if they repeat things, or use long-winded explanations for what they're saying (or believe), people (themselves included) will eventually accept them as fact. The problem is, what people believe and what's actually true, can and often *does* differ.

Repeating incorrect information using aggressive, long, drawn-out statements won't make it correct. This applies to repeating it loudly, as well. If you're wrong, speaking long and loudly doesn't make you *right*. It makes you wrong, long, and *loud!* Consequently, if you're wrong, long, and loud enough times, and do nothing to adjust your behavior, people will eventually add "stupid" to that description. Then... you're wrong, long, loud... and *stupid!* How many people will want you around them, once *those* adjectives have been attached? I could be wrong, but I'm guessing there won't be many.

The point I'm making is there are some surprising explanations for a person not achieving success or happiness. I'm going to be outlining a behavioral pattern throughout the book, but I'm intentionally concealing the punchline, for now. By providing different examples, you should be able to figure it out well before I'm ready to reveal it.

What I *will* say is the person you are, and how you react to the presented circumstances are the reasons you're in the position you're in, whether they're favorable, or unfavorable. They correspond to the thoughts in your head. Only you know the true answers to whom and where you are. As you're reading, you may develop a different perspective on one, or both of them. You may realize you haven't been doing things you *should* have been doing, or you *have* been doing things you *shouldn't* have. This is likely why you're not in your so-called "ideal" position, and why things are the way they are.

Need further assistance in figuring out who you are? Ask someone you trust to describe you, as *they* see you! Sounds easy, but here's the hard part: *tell them you will <u>not</u> interrupt them under any circumstances* until they say, *"I'm done."*

Now, if you ask, you'd better be prepared for any and all responses! It isn't always easy listening to someone tell you about *you*, because you may not like what you hear. This will make it tough to accept, and even tougher to agree with. Truthfully, whether you like it or not, agree or disagree is irrelevant. The question is, *"Can you <u>accept</u> what they tell you, and make adjustments to your behavior, if what they're saying is <u>accurate</u>?"*

An interesting note about communication: It doesn't matter what *you meant*. What matters is how what you meant is *perceived*. This includes your actions as well as your personality. You may see yourself one way, but others perceive you quite differently. You need to understand that your actions and behavior communicate a distinct message, but the message's interpretation is determined, once again, by the perception of the person on the *receiving* end. Think about your most frequent actions and behavior. What could they be saying?

Here's another valuable lesson I've learned: *"Knowledge always comes from an outside entity, but <u>behavior</u> always originates in your head. The key is figuring out which one is pulling the train!"*

3. The Comfort Zone

One of the biggest motivators for me in writing this book is my concern for the future generations of adults. They may be children, tweens, teens, and young adults right now, but they won't stay that way, forever.

Nearly everything in our society has gone haywire, if you blindly buy into the stories depicted in the media, often orchestrated by conspiracy theorists, religious zealots and their supporters, or a number of politicians and *their* supporters. The constant barrage of crime and violence, protests and counter-protests, national debt, global power, human rights debates, and political differences can be quite depressing. Turning on the news each day is a crap-shoot.

If we don't do our part to teach young people the *proper* lessons we were taught by *our* elders, our society is on a collision course with epic failure. Notice I put an emphasis on the word, "proper." Of course, we can't place all the blame on young folks. Sometimes, we "seasoned" folks assume everyone already knows these lessons, but tend to forget that everyone isn't raised the same way. I designed this book not only to educate those who need to learn the lessons, but as a refresher for those of us who don't know how, or may have forgotten how to teach them.

The bulk of society's issues are due to many people's willingness to accept what they're told as gospel. Additionally, many people will take the portion of a situation or statement that triggers their reaction, and they'll run with it, when the appropriate and more *effective* action would be taking the time to get the entire story before reacting. This tends to happen because many people only listen long enough to *respond*... not to *understand*.

Generally speaking, people aren't as quick to do their own research. Instead, they're content with relying on the efforts of other people, assuming they've done *their* research, and that research has resulted in accurate information. I wouldn't discard that statement just yet – you'll see it, again!

The gullibility of people is illustrated repeatedly, if we measure by the many general reactions to what's reported. Too often, people immediately react to a headline, or react to a situation without fact-checking it, first. A select few will also react loudly, but you just read in the last chapter how speaking loudly when you're wrong can turn out.

From this standpoint, the headlines brilliantly do what they were designed to do – attract attention and trigger a reaction. Ideally, a person is supposed to read the headline, become intrigued, then read the article body to get the full story, in that order. Unfortunately, our society is *hardly* ideal.

In this society we've settled so comfortably into, many people choose to accept the headline as the story, and prematurely react. This is partly why I believe instant gratification has done more damage than was originally anticipated. The need for it has become such a large priority, that it often adversely affects a person's rationality.

Many people prefer to focus their attention on an action. Why? An action is easy to condemn! It's right on the surface, indisputable, and easily identifiable. Unfortunately, focusing on the action means the *reason* for it goes largely ignored. The reason can be tough, because of the possibility of discovering their actions may have caused another person's actions. Not everyone can handle that, so the path of least resistance is zeroing in on the action – the *much easier* target!

This collective behavior is a windfall for media outlets. It's one of the main reasons the media keeps feeding the public "morsels" of news. It's also why satire news sources thrive. These entities know morsels leave a lot to the imagination of the "Headline Reactor," which in turn, brews controversy. This translates to the ratings media outlets are constantly seeking. The more controversial a story, the more engaged the audience is. How did you *think* they established their followings? This strategy wasn't invented yesterday!

Life's events operate more or less on this same principle. You're provided morsels of knowledge by other people, and not because they want you to constantly come to them for answers. Well some might, but the majority believe they'll provide the only answer you'll need, or want. Things get murky when you're arranging those morsels into an action plan that can be executed to your advantage.

Every person wants, and deserves a life they can enjoy whether that's meeting great people, buying the things they desire, going on exotic vacations, or engaging in pleasurable activities. In their home, they want to feel safe and peaceful.

When they're able to do this, I think most people would categorize this as achieving a comfortable level of success.

Here's where things get a bit dicey for some folks. You can have the desire, but if you want to *experience* that life, you must be willing to do what's necessary to achieve it. This can be tricky, because right below success is where content resides, and many people live their lives here. In most cases it's perfectly fine, but content can be misleading. It can create a false sense of accomplishment where the characteristics of content are identified, but are somehow mistaken for success.

Some people will argue that content is what we should strive for. I won't debate the concept much, because in its purest form, by definition, content means being in a state of satisfaction, or peaceful happiness. In this context, it's impossible to dispute. However, there's one thing I want to draw your attention to, and it's what I mentioned at the beginning of the 2nd chapter about your thinking and resolving issues. One of the main goals of this book, and an important key in evolving and overcoming obstacles, is getting you to look at situations from a different perspective.

My mind processes things a little differently, as you'll see, the further you read in this book. One of those things is my definition of content. My definition of content means you have everything you want, and no desire to obtain anything else. This means according to *my* off-the-wall thinking, very few people can say they're truly content. Using my definition and context, for those who *aren't* content, an adjustment or two may be warranted.

I will say this: if content *satisfies* you, there's no need to change anything. The decisions you've made thus far have worked for you, and you shouldn't change something if it's working. Any attempt to alter this process can be viewed as trying to *"fix something that ain't broke."*

Here's something I discovered, and believe many people would benefit by burning it into their memory: *"You didn't arrive at your current position by accident."* That may have caught a few people off-guard, so I'll repeat it: *"You didn't arrive at your current position by accident."* What does this mean?

You arrived at your current position by *choice*, not by *chance*. I'll argue until there's no breath left in my body, that where you presently are is the direct result of a series of entangled circumstances. Furthermore, whether that result has been positive or negative, will depend on the decisions you've made to get you to the point you're at.

Even subtle decisions usually taken for granted can alter a person's path to success and happiness. They normally don't spark earth-shattering responses, so we don't give them much thought. However, each decision has made its own unique contribution in putting you where you are.

What if you don't *like* where you are? What can you do? Here's a simple solution: stop, make a slight turn, and start moving again. Know what you're doing, now? You're moving in a *completely different* direction!

This is where many people get tripped up. They don't realize how *easy* changing directions is, or they've decided adjustments are needed, but are afraid to initiate them. Due to complacency, or possibly from being pissed off, they stay where things are familiar. This way, they can justify their behavior, and be able to live with the decision.

Change isn't always easy to embrace, but personal growth cannot be achieved *without* change! Improvement requires some type of change in *every* case, but when a warranted change isn't received favorably, the *necessity* for it is devalued, or ignored. This is *how* a life stagnates, but uncovering *why* it stagnates is much more entertaining.

Primarily, there are two reasons a person's life becomes stagnant. The first is because they *refuse* to listen to anybody. Simply put, they think they *know* everything! In this sense, they're not much different from the arrogant person.

This is ironic when you consider that learning *comes* from listening. Every single thing you've ever learned in life has occurred *when your mouth was shut!* Care to argue with that? The only thing anyone has learned *anything* from running their mouth, is when they can, and cannot run their mouth.

If we know learning comes from listening, then why the refusal to do more of it? Generally, it's because people aren't very receptive to a contradictory point of view. They prefer to live in a state where *their* beliefs are correct, and anyone who opposes or questions those beliefs is *incorrect*. Therefore, that person must be vilified, confronted, mocked, ridiculed, or destroyed in defense of those beliefs. It circles back to being judgmental, and can be viewed as narcissistic to a degree, but also sets the person up for a lot of disappointment.

Many people (particularly arrogant people) will find this hard to accept: *"As much as you'd like to think you do, you don't know everything! You aren't right all the time. Sometimes, you're dead wrong, and when you are, you have to own it!"* Regardless of your education level, unless you invented a process or subject, there's someone who knows it differently (and possibly *better*) than you. Your idea isn't always the best, so get over yourself!

Part of the self-assessment process is learning how to request, but more importantly, *accept* assistance if you determine it's needed. Many times, a person's ego prevents this, due to the uneasy feeling created by the fear of appearing weak or incompetent. This is how easily something created in a person's head can cause them to turn away from actions and information that may actually help them progress.

A by-product of the refusal to listen is the second reason a person's life stagnates. They become content with living in what I refer to as *"The Comfort Zone."* This is a powerful force in many people's lives, and one of the biggest hindrances to their quest for success, but what exactly is it?

Loosely defined, the comfort zone is a person's safe haven. It's their shield. Inside their comfort zone, a person feels protected. If they ever feel their well-being is threatened, they know a retreat to the comfort zone means refuge. This is why many people lean on it so heavily.

I'm not suggesting that you don't *have* a comfort zone. In fact, you need one to develop the confidence to handle success. You must know how far you can push yourself before you get antsy. The comfort zone defines that threshold and keeps you mindful of your limits. The issue with many people is they remain at a particular comfort level much longer than they should, and subconsciously create barriers to their success.

Are you prone to excessively living within your comfort zone? Ponder these two questions: *"Am I truly happy with my current situation?"* and *"Can I identify my comfort zone?"* While you're contemplating your answers to these, I'll again stress the importance of self-honesty. If you can't achieve that, you're never going to uncover a reason to change anything.

If you're dissatisfied with your life, and indeed want to initiate a turnaround, the first step is acknowledging the dissatisfaction. It's like a 12-step program for addiction. Recovery starts with admitting that at the moment, the problem is stronger than you. Continuing to reject the need for adjustments keeps you on your current course, which, if you decided you're not satisfied, *"ain't where you want to be!"* What's remarkable is many people remain where they don't want to be for a variety of reasons – most likely because it's familiar. In essence, complacency *becomes* the comfort zone.

I've adopted a philosophy that helps me get through many of life's stumbling blocks: *"If you can identify an issue well enough to tell another person about it, then you have the ability to resolve the issue."* You'll need knowledge and diligence. Do nothing and you risk repeating current decisions, as well as not altering the situation you said you're dissatisfied with!

Albert Einstein was considered by many people to be a genius. He's credited with defining insanity as repeating the same action, but expecting a different result. The statement (made in 1951 by most accounts) still resonates today, though the meaning has been grossly misinterpreted.

Doing something repeatedly becomes a routine. A routine is eventually deemed safe because you know the end result, from doing it so many times. For example, if you've worked at a job for 20 years, you're familiar with nearly every aspect of that job. It's part of your routine. You get used to the situation, and normally function without worry. Any disruption to that routine is usually met with a degree of anxiety, because you may be oblivious to the fact that an action must change to achieve a different result.

I'm not saying quit a great job you've had for 20 years! I'm using it as an illustration of how easy it can be to fall into the comfort zone trap. Working at a job for 20 years is *not* insane, but working at a job for 20 years and making no attempts to improve it might be teetering on the insanity platform. The *job* might not need to improve… *you* might!

Going through our daily routines, we see people we'd categorize as "successful" and wonder why success skipped us. We see them on television, or other form of media, and wonder, *"Why is this person famous? What has this no talent-having person done that I have not, and why have the success Gods picked them to smile on, instead of me?"* It's okay to admit it. I had to!

It's imperative to understand, every successful person wasn't born with a silver spoon in their mouth. Few people are *born* into success. The majority had to earn it, and began with little more than a dream. What separated them was their willingness to step out of their comfort zone to do something unfamiliar, *despite* the obstacles they encountered.

My career in the Air Force taught me countless lessons. This isn't an attempt to convince anyone that the Air Force is a great opportunity, though it worked wonders for me. I'm simply pointing out that many of life's most impactful lessons can come from the most unlikely sources.

If I had to pick one characteristic that I've developed effectively, I'd be hard-pressed to say it isn't logic. I say developed because I've always been a logical thinker. Logic has allowed me to deal with issues more confidently. It's also the trait about me that makes people most upset, because there aren't many things that get me riled up. I believe there is a logical explanation for everything we experience.

Before I decided on the Air Force as a career, I received guidance from family and friends that really tested my logic. I was fortunate to have my great-grandmother until I was almost 30 years old, and she was an amazing woman! *Mean as a snake, but sharp as a tack!* I remember her talking about her experiences, foolishly thinking it was for my entertainment. I soon realized she was preparing me for an unrelenting world. I was getting an education a school couldn't teach!

One of the most profound lessons I learned from her, was if I wanted things to *turn out* differently, I needed to *do* things differently. If I did what everyone else did, I wouldn't stand out. I'd be like everybody else, and logically, I shouldn't expect a different result. Her message to me was simple: set a goal, and don't let anyone but *you* stop you from achieving it.

As long as you're not hurting yourself or anyone else in the process, go after any and every goal you want.

I grew up in Oakland. If you've ever lived in, or heard stories about Oakland (or any larger city, for that matter), you know it can be a rough place. Probably more so now, but Oakland was a rough place to grow up during the 1970s and 80s. Many of today's issues existed back then. One of the major differences between then and now is the community's collective acceptance and response to these issues. With that, I want to take you to my childhood for a moment. Not for a history lesson, but to highlight some of the events that have helped shape my ideology.

One of the most vivid memories I have is when I was about 10 years old. For about a year or so, I only saw my dad on the weekends. It wasn't because he was inactive in my life. He worked a 3:30pm to midnight shift at his job. As a result, he was asleep when I left for school, gone to work when I came home from school, and I was asleep when *he* came home from work.

On the weekends we talked about a lot of things. That means he would talk, and I'd *act* like I was listening! Tossing out an agreement here and there and nodding my head a lot to what he was saying seemed logical in my immature mind. Of course, as a child, I wasn't overly concerned with learning any of life's lessons.

Like most children, I thought my parents were idiots. They'd never been my age, and couldn't possibly know what I was going through. It sounds stupid to say now, but hey...

that's a child's rationale! Most of what my parents said was filed under the "nonsense" category in my brain – in one ear and out the other. I can remember frequently saying, *"They don't know what the hell they're talkin' about!"* I was walking away, muttering it under my breath every time... but I *said* it!

My epiphany came when I was about 22 years old. I was nearing the end of my enlistment in the Air Force and planning my next move. I needed to decide whether to re-enlist, or separate from service. By this time, I had family responsibilities, and was no longer thinking for only myself. Whatever my decision was, it would affect other lives.

One day out of nowhere, reality hit me like a ton of bricks had dropped on my head! It suddenly dawned on me: my parents were *not* stupid! But just think... up to that point, I'd insisted, and truly tried to make myself believe they *were!* What was actually happening was the information they'd been drilling into my head was starting to make sense.

It's hard to describe the feeling of finally grasping a life lesson that had been eluding you. It's like a breath of fresh air first thing in the morning. Your head becomes clear; your eyes wide open. I decided to re-enlist and the rest is history.

Do you remember the question asked a few pages ago: *"Am I truly happy with my situation?"* A percentage of people will emphatically tell you they *are*. That's great! If you fall into this category, you may feel like skipping to the next chapter. However, here's an interesting yet humorous observation: if you've read this far into the chapter, it won't hurt you to finish it. Besides, you're already more than halfway through it!

If you're like me, you fall into the *"For the most part I'm satisfied, but things can always be better"* category. Most people feel this way, but there are people who aren't happy with much of their situation and would change a number of things about it, if given the chance. I can't count the times I've heard people say they want to change their circumstances but are unable to find a way to do it. What I've found is a number of these people aren't *unable* to initiate the changes – they're *unwilling*.

Where many people fail, and add self-inflicted stress to their lives, is they refuse (yes, I said *refuse*) to acknowledge the fact that circumstances *can't* be changed! Instead of adjusting their behavior to fit the circumstances, they expect the *circumstances* to adjust, to fit *their behavior.*

Circumstances are inanimate. They are what they are. If you're standing in the path of a falling rock, the rock is falling toward you, whether you want it to, or not. You can't change the path of the rock, but you *can* change *where you stand!*

This is why so many people get stuck in their comfort zone. They get caught spinning their wheels, trying to change something that can't be changed, and end up launching their attacks at the wrong target. You can't control circumstances, but your reaction to them is *completely* within your control.

"There are extraordinary people in our society." Most people have heard a variation of this, but I have the feeling what I say next is going to prompt a few frowns: I don't believe the statement is true. Yes, you read that correctly! I don't believe there are extraordinary people. I believe there are ordinary people who do extraordinary things, and there are countless

examples of it: the neighborhood nurse who treats everyone's cuts, scrapes, and bruises; the teacher who stays at work to help a struggling student; the high school senior leading the charge for raising money for breast cancer research, after her mother passed away from it.

None of these people set out to be a hero. They were motivated to do the things they did by a feeling that they could make a positive impact on another person's life through their actions. It just so happens that those actions were described by *other* people as being "extraordinary."

These people obviously didn't possess a super power, so what was it that motivated their actions? They were willing to go against the grain. The point I'm making is many of the things we've seen, and classified as extraordinary may not have occurred if everyone stayed within their comfort zones.

Many of the sticking points people face in life can be attributed to a small word. This is going to sound absurd when you read it, but one tiny word has been responsible for the stifling of a person's progress, in many cases. It's been extremely successful at its job, and will continue to be, as long as people choose to remain in the dark about its power.

Are you holding on to your seat? Great! The word is *no*. That's right - *no!* It sounds ridiculous, doesn't it!? It's inconceivable to think such a small word could create so much turmoil, but here's my argument to support what I said.

"No" is a safe response when an idea or task is unfamiliar to you. Why? Up to that point, the idea or task hasn't helped, nor hurt you. As long as you continue saying *"no,"* you remain in your comfort zone and feel protected. Why shouldn't you? Everything in there is familiar.

Here's the major *flaw* with this thinking. Remaining in the comfort zone means things never change, *because* everything in there is familiar! If everyone said no to every foreign-sounding or unfamiliar request, the world would be nowhere. We'd be stuck in an endless abyss of complacency. Let's look at an event from the 1800s as an example. I'm certain it was more complex than this, but stay with me.

Someone realized they couldn't complete their day's activities before the sun set, and the moon didn't provide enough light for them to work at night. They needed a device that allowed them to see at night, have both hands free, and didn't pose as much of a risk of fire as a torch would.

They didn't feel they had the ability to create something like that themselves, but remembered Thomas Edison dabbled in a lot of scientific activity, and requested his assistance. Had Mr. Edison answered *no* to their request, light bulbs would not have been invented at the time they were!

I'm certain someone else would have come up with the idea had Mr. Edison declined, but an important moment in history would have been altered, and what would be the culprit? A 2-letter word you don't even need to *move your lips* to say! You just checked to see if you could do it, didn't you?!

What's the moral of the story? To do something *extraordinary,* you must be willing to *separate* yourself from ordinary. Mr. Edison decided to step out of his comfort zone and take a shot at the impossible. He set a goal to create a working light bulb, and failed 2,000 times in the process. He persisted when the average person may have given up. Incidentally, something extremely interesting happened on that *2001*st attempt...

What I'm saying is there are times when you simply have to throw caution to the wind, and take a leap of faith. It can be a scary thought, but saying *no* creates self-imposed limits to your progress. To me, that's an even scarier thought! In many instances, people have become grounded to their comfort zone because of fear of the unknown, or worse, of failure. As a result, they say no. Instead of being so quick to say *no*, try switching things up, and say *"maybe."* This small gesture may be just what you need to get you out of a rut.

Saying you want to change, and initiating the change are two different things. You must be willing to get off your butt and do something, because making a decision to change is only the beginning. Logically speaking, talking only produces noise. Action is what gets the ball moving. A sports reference is an appropriate way to transition to the next paragraph.

Michael Jordan is arguably the greatest basketball player to play in the NBA. His unique athletic ability changed the game of basketball in such a way, that many of today's top players pattern their playing style after his. He played amazingly well, but he wasn't born that way.

According to stories I've read, Mr. Jordan didn't initially make his high school varsity team. At the time, the coach felt he wasn't skilled enough to play at that level. Had he chosen to remain within the boundaries of his comfort zone, we may have never seen him play in the NBA. Fortunately for the basketball world, he used that rejection as fuel to improve.

Those who have seen him play might be surprised to learn that his career shooting percentage is 49.5% (NBA Encyclopedia - Playoff Edition, 2016). He missed *over half* the shots he took! Despite this "less than stellar" performance, you'd be hard-pressed to find an NBA enthusiast who would *not* put him in their top-10 list of all-time best players.

One trait made him stand out: determination. He used the obstacles he encountered (coaches, other players, etc.), as motivation. What are the results of his efforts? How about six NBA championships, six NBA Finals Most Valuable Player awards, five NBA Most Valuable Player awards, two Olympic gold medals, and enshrinement in the NBA Hall of Fame, among numerous other awards.

Whether he truly *is* the greatest is a matter of opinion, and I'm not going to debate the issue. There are too many great players throughout history to make such a declaration. *Your* greatest player may be different, and that's perfectly fine. Truthfully, it doesn't matter.

When all is said and done, Michael Jordan is a man with faults and flaws, just like everyone else. Whether you like or dislike him, agree or disagree with anything he says or does is *irrelevant*. What I want you to appreciate is how persistence can pay off when a person refuses to accept their current circumstances as their destiny, and has the guts to find another path to achieve a goal they've set for themselves.

Hold on a second. Is that the *end all, be all?* Does *believing* you can do something guarantee you'll be successful at doing it? Absolutely not, but it's a great start! It's going to take that belief, along with effort, persistence, and few other things you'll read about in other chapters.

Along the road to success, there's bound to be failure. It's inevitable. I can't think of one successful person who got *everything* right on their first attempt. I suppose it's possible, but highly unlikely. This begs the question, *"Why should I try something if I know from the beginning that I might fail at it?"*

Well, for starters, how about because you may *not* fail?! That should be reason *enough*, but secondly, because you shouldn't be afraid of failure. Failure is a wonderful teacher, if you pay attention to the lessons it teaches. In many instances, failure can be a catalyst to success. Normally, failure isn't the issue. The issue is what a person *does* when they encounter failure. Many people use the moment of failure as a reason to discard their goal.

The person undeterred by the possibility of failure is usually the one who succeeds. I've provided two examples with Mr. Einstein and Mr. Jordan respectively, but here are a few more: Oprah Winfrey was passed over because producers felt she was unfit for television. A record executive told multiple-time Grammy Award-winner Anita Baker that she couldn't sing. Bill Gates and Paul Allen failed *several* times before successfully launching Microsoft! Each of these situations ultimately unfolded quite differently than the original rejecters of these people may have predicted.

The common denominator shared by these folks was dissatisfaction with their circumstances at the time. They each had a belief in themselves, and the courage to step out of their comfort zone. They refused to allow even the possibility of failing dampen their will to succeed. If they had, we may have never been witness to their talents and/or contributions.

The difference between remaining in and breaking away from your comfort zone is dictated by your reaction to the presented circumstances. Your reaction is the result of a perception which is heavily influenced by your mindset, and is created entirely *in your head* (I said you'd see that, again).

The perception *you create* often determines your success or failure at a task. For example, tell yourself something's *"gonna suck,"* and it's *"gonna suck!"* Saying something is *"gonna suck"* without first assessing the situation, can cause you to form a preconceived outcome, and literally defeat yourself before the game starts.

One of the best pieces of wisdom I've ever received was from a former supervisor. Ever since the day I heard it, I've held it in high regard, and it has become one of my absolute favorite sayings: *"You can find a million reasons not to do something, but only need to find one reason to do it."*

People are naturally resistant to unfamiliar ideas and tasks. This is one of the reasons comfort zones are so prevalent. Within your comfort zone, you're the boss. You know how to handle things thrown at you, because it's familiar domain. Learning to step away from your comfort zone without fear of it not being there exposes you to different perspectives. The important thing to remember is everything *unfamiliar* to you isn't *detrimental* to you!

It is perfectly acceptable to be prepared for the unexpected, but you don't have to expect it around every corner. You're going to drive yourself insane if you become comfortable with being *"perpetually defensive."* What is the point of walking around with your fists balled up? Because something *might* happen? What if nothing happens? Then, you will have spent an enormous amount of time looking for something that wasn't there to begin with. All of this is thanks to something you create in your own head!

There is such a thing as being *too* cautious. Constantly being on the lookout for things to defend yourself against not only adds unnecessary stress to ordinary situations, but has to be *mind-numbingly* exhausting! However, you are the *only* one with the power to alter your reaction to a given situation.

The bottom line is if you want to make purposeful and positive adjustments to your life, you'll need to have enough faith, knowledge, and confidence in your ability to know you can function effectively, without relying heavily on your comfort zone. Taking the first step outside of it will be the most difficult. Subsequent steps will get easier as you grow more comfortable with being away from it, but first, you need to get your feet moving. If you've never fallen down before, you have no idea of how great it feels to get back up!

4. A Fear of Winning

"Wait... *what?!* A fear of winning?" I'm sure a few people read the title of this chapter and immediately thought, *"What in the world is he talking about? I like winning! Winning is the goal of playing a game, isn't it? How can someone have a fear of winning? You'll have to explain this one, Kevin."* I'd be happy to.

First, don't misinterpret the chapter's title, and make the assumption that I believe winning is *bad*. Winning isn't bad! I don't know anyone who would argue that it is, and I won't be "that guy." I suppose anything is possible, but I have *yet* to come across a happy, successful *loser*.

Winning is a critical element in the success and living happy formula. Two other traits belong in that formula: *truth* and *logic*. These two are essential to my preferred method of communicating, and I depend heavily on both. While we're discussing truth, many people *say* they prefer the truth, but after observing a number of them, I wonder if they really *do?!*

Truth is a hard pill to swallow. Why? It has a well-known ability to absolutely *crush* a person's beliefs! This is why many people choose to tread lightly, or dance around it. To aid them in doing this, a person may intentionally create distractions in an effort to blur the focus of a situation. They'll try to dominate a situation by flooding it with radical-sounding ideas, slanted propaganda, aggressive terms and demeanor, long, drawn-out statements, or graphic images designed to shock, or wear a person down. This is done with a specific purpose in mind: triggering an emotional reaction.

I've figured out, when a person is displaying this type of behavior, *the* truth isn't really what they're looking for. What they're really looking for is *their* truth coming out of another person's mouth! This is known as *validation*, which will be discussed in a later chapter.

To my interpretation, there are two types of people when it comes to dealing with truth. One faces the truth, and accepts it for what it is. They use it to their advantage by making adjustments to their behavior, to best suit the situation. The other refuses to acknowledge truth, no matter how overwhelming the evidence may be. The latter is the person who prefers living within those figurative walls, because it's their safe haven. Every fact in the world could be staring them in their face, and they'd *still* ignore them!

"Well, the truth is what it is, right? Why not accept it as it is, and move on?" I couldn't agree more! Truth is absolute, and realistically, there's no argument against the truth except a *ridiculous* one. So, accepting the truth seems logical to the level-headed person, but people are individually-wired. Not everyone *is* level-headed. There are people who simply don't (or won't) accept truth as it is. Instead, they try to *manipulate* truth into something they will *accept!* Why? The lie (because that's what it *is*, if it's not truth) is easier for them to digest.

Hold on. If truth is absolute, then why would a person have a hard time accepting it? An explanation for this can be complicated. I'll attempt one by offering an illustration of how refusing to acknowledge truth may be what's creating unnecessary obstacles on the path to improvement. My explanation may also clarify some things, if you discover you're one of those people who have trouble accepting truth.

Many people become what I refer to as *"paralyzed by fear."* In them, fear emerges as the dominant emotion, and it makes them uncomfortable. To compensate for the fear, the person creates a façade. They form a barrier of excuses (not to be confused with reasons) for something not getting done, and hide behind it. They do everything possible to convince themselves everything is fine as it appears. This behavior is *also* remarkably similar to that of the arrogant person.

Unfortunately, this paves the way for some severe consequences, because the person suffering from the condition may not realize they're exhibiting the behavior. Others know they're exhibiting it, but are unable to pinpoint *why* they're remaining in their state. They'll be able to recognize some potential "whys" by the end of this chapter!

The paralysis (as I've labeled it) is created when fear, for whatever reason, is strong enough to motivate a person to intentionally engage in what I call *"self-sabotage."* This is likely due to a feeling that something they've been looking for is missing. The deeper the feeling is, the more immersed in the behavior they become. This is their method of compensating for the thing they believe is missing, and leads to behavior or actions that keep them running on a hamster wheel, by creating the *illusion* of achievement or satisfaction. In reality, the action or behavior does nothing to challenge them to engage in activity designed to help them get, or stay ahead.

Studies and practical experience have shown certain behavioral actions do more harm than good. The amazing thing is most people are aware of the destructive results of these actions, but many are unaware of the chain of events they can trigger. This is why I've termed it "*self*-sabotage."

It sounds ridiculous to think a person would *intentionally* engage in activity they know won't end well, but if we look at the antics of a number of people, you have to wonder, *"Is it really <u>ridiculous</u>, if the activities are happening more frequently?"* Why would a person do such things if they know they won't end well? It justifies their actions and behavior. More on this later.

I want to direct your attention to illegal drug use. This is discussed in another chapter, but I'll save you the trouble of looking for it right now, by giving you a brief preview. There are other vices that detour people off the path to success, but this is an easy one I can use to make my point.

There are people who use drugs, but far too many people wind up abusing them. With the amount of research that has been done on drug usage and abuse, it's common knowledge that people will become addicted if they use drugs long enough. Yet many people are willing to gamble that they *won't* use them long enough. The problem is, "long enough" differs with each person! See? *Self*-sabotage!

The term *addict* can just as easily be used to describe the drug dealer, as well. Of course in most cases, the dealer's addiction isn't to the drugs themselves. Their addiction is to the by-products stemming from the drugs: money, cars, houses, jewelry, women (or men, depending on preference), the power they feel, or the fear people appear to have of them. At least one of these is providing the adrenaline that's fueling their desire to continue the activity.

In addition to drugs, there are people who engage in other criminal activities as their method of gaining prosperity. Some people make a choice to participate, while others are heavily influenced or pressured into it. Usually the decision is based on the person's desire to feel important, protected, included, or accepted. Regardless of reasoning, drugs, gangs, and other crimes are fairly common no matter where you live.

While those activities are fresh in your mind, here's another rhetorical question: How many 50 or 60-year old drug users, dealers, or gang members can you think of? Take it a step further and lower the age to 45. Can't think of many? That's the point – there *aren't* many! Usually people in this demographic who have chosen to participate in these activities either no longer *personally* engage in them, are incarcerated, or unfortunately, have passed away.

I say usually because as with any rule, there have always been, and will always be exceptions. Some of the most "successful" criminals were over 50 years old when they met their demise, whether it was incarceration, injury, or death. Many may still operate today, though if they do, I seriously doubt they're directly involved in the activity. They've learned to create distance between them and the activity. Otherwise, they would have suffered an unfortunate demise a while back.

You may be wondering if these types of activities have unfolded tragically rather than favorably in so many cases, why a person would frequently put their well-being at risk by engaging in them?! Their decisions and actions are driven by what they have in their head.

They're convinced that the overwhelming evidence of people suffering horrible demises as a result of these activities is somehow slanted. Tragedy will bypass them. *They* will be the person who, despite many that have failed before them, defies the odds and disproves the evidence. *They* will be part of the few who've achieved long-term success while engaging in activities *not* designed for long-term success. From the outside looking in, this sounds crazy, but this is what has to happen in order for a person to choose this route.

Hold on… their confidence in their ability is actually a *good* thing! It's just being applied in the wrong context. Their behavior displays persistence, another important component of success. From this standpoint, they possess two valuable characteristics. It's now a matter of expanding and building on them, because they have an identifiable starting point.

Along with confidence and persistence, there must be logic and reason. It's about knowing the difference between *possibility* and *probability*. There's a *possibility* of a long, safe, happy life while constantly engaging in these activities, but history and statistics have shown scores of examples where that hasn't happened. *Probability* doesn't favor the philosophy.

Somewhere in the person's mind, a battle of brain cells takes place. When they repeatedly choose criminal activity, it shouldn't be hard to figure out which side prevails. The variable that's missing is when they will be caught. Notice I didn't say *if*, but *when!* If they haven't been caught, yet continue these activities, capture *is* coming. It's inevitable!

Of course, no one sets *out* with the intent of getting caught. People participate in these activities because they plan to *get away* with them! What I'm pointing out is there are few positive outcomes, compared to negative ones. Even people who regularly participate in these activities will tell you longevity isn't something they think about often, because they know history and statistics don't support a longevity theory.

In their mind, it's easier to toss the odds aside, and place their bets on hope. They *hope* they don't meet a horrible, premature demise. They *hope* they live long enough to find another way of getting the things they want before an enemy, family member, or friend contributes to their downfall.

While this mentality may work for some people, when it comes to *my* success, I'm not willing to take that kind of a gamble with *hope* as my currency! That's like firing a weapon with your eyes closed. You can only *hope* to hit your target.

This isn't knocking those who believe criminal activity is necessary. Some feel it's necessary for survival. For others, it may be the only way they know. They may not have been exposed to the safer (and legal) alternatives that achieve the same results, just not as fast. For whatever reason, they've grown comfortable with their current activities. Wait a minute... was that another comfort zone reference?!

The truth is people will do what they feel is necessary to make the best of the situation they're in. However, an unfortunate but *undeniable* reality of criminal activity (a "gangs, drugs, and hustling are the easiest and quickest ways to prosperity" mentality), is incarceration, injury, and death are far more common outcomes than living happily ever after. You must understand this *before* choosing criminal activity as your route. This way, when and if those things happen, you aren't surprised! You'll know exactly why they're happening.

What about people who *don't* engage in criminal activity, per se? Can they be guilty of self-sabotage? *Abso-freakin'-lutely!* These people aren't just a danger to themselves, but to others, as well. Why is that? It's because unlike the person who willingly participates in criminal activity, the person who does not, most likely will not see anything wrong with their behavior. In their eyes, they must be okay because they're not breaking the law. Whether they are or not is debatable, as you'll soon see.

This person is likely unaware that they're inadvertently derailing themselves off the track to success. They've become so paralyzed, they're convinced "just getting by" is acceptable. They've gotten stuck. Improving their situation requires them getting *un*-stuck, and perhaps this book can provide the "grease" to help *get* them un-stuck.

So, who *is* this paralyzed person? I'm certain you've seen or heard of them. It might even be *you!* The paralyzed person does their best to put up a front, to appear successful to others. Some of the things they do defy logic in many people's minds, but are done to portray a successful persona to outside eyes. Unfortunately the persona is nothing but an illusion, but it's so convincing, it even fools the person trying to *live it!* You think I'm kidding? The following are a few examples of this behavior exhibited by paralyzed people. See if anyone you know fits one of these descriptions, and you can decide for *yourself* if the persona has them fooled or not.

The person lives paycheck to paycheck, often relying on others' generosity to sustain their well-being. They have little desire to do *anything* outside of their comfort zone (there it is, again!), and are perfectly content with making no efforts to do so. In their eyes, the status quo is adequate. You hear more *talk* from them about what they're going to do than action from them actually *doing* what they say they want to do.

They drive a $60,000 car, but have no garage to park it because they're *renting* an apartment! Or they have pictures of themselves on social media enjoying expensive meals and drinks like there's no tomorrow, but they're living in someone *else's* house without even *offering* to pay any of the household expenses. They spend $65 on alcohol 1-2 times a week, but it's usually gone the same day they buy it, because they're drinking it with five other people. They buy designer clothes for babies that won't fit for more than two weeks.

This is commonly referred to as "turning up," but turning up for whom? Is it for other people, or for themselves? It certainly isn't for the babies, because they don't know enough to care about designer clothes. Food, play, bath time, potty, and sleep are the staples of a baby's day. They couldn't care less about the name on their clothes!

The paralyzed person has no problem doing any of the things described above, but seems to have a *major* problem with registering for a course at a local college. Do the math: college course fees are approximately $140, while two $65 bottles of alcohol is $130. The cost of the bottles could be part of a self-investment that results in increased education and never goes away. A buzz or high is gone in about two hours! So, is it really the *circumstances* doing them in? *Nope*, their *mindset* is the problem! There it is again – *self*-sabotage!

At the other end of the spectrum are the people who spend their time inventing ways to beat the system. I guess in some ways, this would border criminal activity. These people spin their wheels finding ways to get something for nothing.

They fake injuries or illnesses to receive disability payments because they're unwilling to work a legitimate job. They put utilities in a family member's name, and then don't pay the bill. They don't answer the phone to avoid bill collectors, as if *ignoring* the bill somehow makes it not exist, or they duck and dodge the property manager on rent day.

In affluent communities these types of things rarely happen, though I put nothing passed anyone, but in middle or lower class communities, they're not uncommon. I grew up calling it "getting over." More recently, it's being referred to as a "come up." Regardless of what it's called, it describes a person unwilling to put forth the necessary effort for positive personal gain. Instead, they look for a shortcut.

Ambition is overshadowed by content, and if they believe their shortcut is successful, it creates the false sense of accomplishment.

The situation is amplified if the person has *enablers*. These unsuspecting people may be genuinely trying to help, but their efforts usually end up having the opposite effect. They hinder the paralyzed person's progress by providing them a crutch or safety net. This reinforces the comfort zone, giving them permission to continue the behavior.

These descriptions don't paint flattering images, and likely made a number of *guilty* people uncomfortable reading them. I deliberately worded them the way I did, to make a point. There are people in society who legitimately need assistance. Unfortunately, because of the people who intentionally take advantage of the system for their own selfish benefit, they can't get the assistance they need.

The troubling thing is, instead of finding out what makes them better, many paralyzed people opt for the path of least resistance and stay where they are. They believe their current way of living is okay because it has become their routine. The part they *don't* see is they've unknowingly sold themselves short and fallen victim to an *"invented reality."* Consequently, they've gotten into the practice of accepting mediocrity, and mistaking content for success.

I was one of those paralyzed people. I didn't engage in drugs or criminal activity, but I *was* guilty of selling myself short, for a long time. In spite of the guidance I'd been given, I managed to convince myself that on some level, mediocrity was acceptable. I found it acceptable, but that doesn't mean I was comfortable with my acceptance. I've never viewed myself as mediocre, but I definitely had a fear of winning.

I chose to process my fear as a lot of people do. I ignored the truth, let the issues fester, and hoped they'd improve if I left them alone. I retreated to my comfort zone because it's where I felt safe. I can now recognize that I wasn't *living*. I existed, and there is a big difference.

All of this supports my theory that a paralysis by a fear of winning can prevent a person from achieving success and happiness. Progress is stopped (or stalled) by something in their head. There lies the issue. Now, here's an *antidote*...

For the enabler, the task is easy. One of the *best* things you can do for the paralyzed person (and yourself) is to hand the problem back to *them!* You have your own issues to deal with. Why take on theirs? It may seem harsh, but once they realize the problem is *theirs*, they'll have two options: cower down, or rise to the challenge. Eliminate the middle ground, or safety net, and it's "sink or swim." A person won't change their behavior, until they hit *their* rock bottom... not *yours!*

For the paralyzed person, there's an extremely effective method of conquering this figurative fear of winning. It's something I often say, and logically makes sense. Here's why. The person who receives rewards or luxuries despite making no effort to *earn* them feels as though they're "getting over." They affectionately, but *mistakenly* refer to themselves as *hustlers*. Zero effort is spent, yet a reward is gained. On some level, this satisfies the paralyzed person.

I'll offer this advice for that person, but with another word of caution: If you have the thin skin I mentioned in the first chapter, this is a good time to grab your armor and helmet, because what I'm about to say is going to drop like a sledgehammer: *"Stop trying to get over... and just get <u>better</u>!"*

No matter how good you think you are, you won't be able to "get over" forever. If you have thus far, quite frankly you've been nothing more than lucky, and luck will eventually run out. When it does, you'll find yourself caught in a trap of trying to resolve issues in a panic, which results in rushed judgment or action, and ultimately leads to errant decisions.

What's worse is after all that, if you haven't gotten what you initially wanted, you *still* have to find another method of getting it! *Congratulations...* you've unnecessarily *doubled* your workload, when the aim was to *lessen* it! You're willing to put yourself through that for the sake of believing you're "getting over?!" How silly does "getting over" sound, now?

A far more effective (and less stressful) alternative to "getting over," is getting better. You can always get better at something, and just like the hand up I mentioned in the first chapter, the effects will last longer. Additionally, you won't have to constantly wonder if someone has caught onto your scheme, or is possibly trying to get over on *you*.

Everyone has a desire to win; not everyone is *prepared* to win. It isn't always easy to spot the light at the end of the tunnel, but it *is* there. Success is yours for the taking, but it's not going to be handed to you. It takes an enormous amount of courage to change the course of your life, in order to obtain success, but it *can* be done. You must be willing to go over, under, around, or even *through* any obstacle that happens to be blocking your path to it.

Think about this: everything you want to achieve in life is located just on the other side of fear, pride, and self-doubt! The things you need are the motivation, the methods, and the tools to get you over there.

A great start is removing the thought of being afraid to fail. You're *going* to fail at some tasks, so you might as well accept it. However, the possibility of failure should never deter you from pursuing a goal you want. Failure isn't the end of the line, until you *make* it the end of the line! Use failure as a teacher instead of a roadblock.

Stay focused on the goal, not the obstacle. If you fail but still want to achieve the goal, acknowledge the failure, assess what went wrong, restructure your plan, and attack it from another direction. The goal doesn't change, but your plan to achieve it can *always* change! I mentioned flexibility earlier. *This* is why you need to develop this important trait.

Once you learn to break the cycle of caving in to fear and replace it with faith and confidence in your ability, a new path will be revealed. Fear is much easier to overcome once you realize, you've possessed what was needed to conquer it *all along!* Seriously… it's been there the whole time!

Fear has handicapped you long enough. Stop allowing it to paralyze you. You're only going to continue talking yourself out of making well-deserved progress. You need to put your foot on fear's throat, and tell it to leave you alone while you work. You need to recognize and respect fear, but not *fear* fear. That was *not* a typo, either!

Whether it's being used for good, or for malice, fear is nothing more than a control and manipulation technique employed by religions, parents, teachers, politicians, criminals, terrorists, and bullies. In fact, any entity that has wanted to emphatically seize control of a situation has used fear as their method of doing so. These entities have done an excellent job of getting people to conform to a prescribed way of thinking, because those being controlled haven't found a way to look beyond the fear. In a way, the entity assumes the role of the *oppressor*, meaning it wants to dictate the behavior of the person they want to control, while by default, the person being controlled lands in the role of the *oppressed*.

What's the main message here? There are outside forces *itching* to control you, and their preferred method of trying to do this is through the use of fear. It's how they gain strength, and make their attempts to perpetuate their authority. They know if they can keep you afraid or paranoid, you'll do anything in your power to keep that feeling of fear at bay. They understand if they can keep you scared, they can keep you! You read one of the top reasons they favor this tactic: *it works!* Why help them out by using the tactic on yourself?

Let's put this in another context. Fear is a powerful force. Therefore, it's going to take an even *more* powerful force to defeat it. The battle between striving for success and settling for content, takes place in your head, and the last time

I checked, your head is attached to your body, all day, every day. That means you have *complete* control of it.

The greatest fear for an oppressor is that the oppressed will realize their self-worth, and no longer needs to depend on the *oppressor* for sustainability or validation. When, and if that happens, it's a wrap for the oppressor because the balance of power shifts. The thought of being perceived as insignificant can be *terrifying*. When a person feels terrified, they'll do whatever they need to, even resorting to extreme actions or behavior, in order to make the fearful feeling subside, as you read a few paragraphs back.

A common method used by oppressors to aid in trying to hold on to their *perceived* power, is creating distractions with invented chaos. How this works, is if the oppressed are preoccupied with stopping the *chaos*, or they're fighting and bickering among themselves, they're not as focused on their *progression*. They'll most likely overlook, or miss what the oppressor is doing, and the balance of power shifts back to the oppressor. See how that works? This strategy has worked for ages! To improve, this cycle must be broken.

Here's something else to remember: *"The toughest opponent you will ever face in life… is you!"* One of the best things you can do for yourself is to develop and accept responsibility for your actions. If you can summon the courage to stand up to yourself in situations where fear tries to present *itself*, standing up to an outside force trying to control you with fear will be a *breeze*!

5. Is the Glass Half-Empty, or Half-Full?

Interacting with as many different personalities as I have over the years (and there have been a lot), one thing that has fascinated me is the complexity of the human brain. I find it interesting how a person's brain influences decision-making. It's not interesting enough to motivate me to go to school to become a psychologist or psychiatrist, though. I'm perfectly "content" (intentional reference) with admiring the brain's complexity from afar.

This chapter discusses a practice I've seen many people do on numerous occasions. Each time, I wonder *"Why are they doing this?!"* I'm referring to people who spend a lot of their time complaining about the things that are going, or have gone wrong in their life, yet taking very few (if any) measures to correct the things they're complaining about. This behavior is *beyond* confusing to me.

If you allow them to, they will talk your ear off about every obstacle they believe is preventing them from achieving their goals. Something is always in the way, or someone is sabotaging them. Many times, their explanation is fueled by anger or frustration, which is completely understandable, but after hearing a few of them, I often wonder, *"Okay... and?"*

Did you notice I said *wonder,* and not *say?* I'll explain why you shouldn't *say* such things in a moment, but I've noticed a theme in listening to these people. According to *them*, nearly every obstacle they've encountered has been put there by something, or someone else. I beg to differ.

My parents taught me another painful, but valuable lesson growing up: *"Everything wrong in your life ain't somebody else's fault! Sometimes to find a problem, the place you need to look is in a mirror."* When a person is finding their niche, the comfort zone coupled with the figurative fear of winning will have them looking at every reason under the sun something failed – *except* the reason staring them smack in their face! Why is this? Because, *"As long as I can convince myself that something, or somebody else is the problem... the problem ain't me!"*

I'm certain at some point you've witnessed, or been a part of a scenario similar to the following: an event goes wrong – maybe it's a dent in the car, a broken dish, or whatever, but a person who has been directly affected by the event starts going absolutely *nuts* about it.

During their tirade, you realize nothing can be said or done to calm them down. They aren't listening to what you or anyone else has to say. If you're lucky enough to get a word in edgewise, what you say only fuels the fire. What do you do? If you're like me, you close your mouth, dig in your heels, brace for impact, and ride the storm out.

Once their tirade has subsided (whenever *that* may be), you ask them what got them so angry. Following their explanation, you think, *"Is that it? That's what made you mad? You've got to be kidding! That wasn't severe enough for you to go 5150!"* (5150 is a term that defines unstable or crazy people).

I said *"think,"* and not *"say what you're thinking."* This is a slippery slope to straddle. It can be difficult to bite your tongue in situations like these, but sometimes it's easier and less stressful to allow the tirade to conclude before saying anything. Interruptions may drag it out longer than necessary.

However, don't misinterpret what I'm saying. I'd never advocate discounting another person's feelings. If someone expresses to you that they think a problem exists... *a problem exists!* You are in no position to tell them it doesn't. You're not in their head, and thus, not at liberty to tell them what they see, or *don't* see. Until the person *confirms* the problem no longer exists, it's still there. As the recipient of this information you must treat it as such, and without judgment.

Another thing that confuses me is how people manage to make situations more difficult than they need to be, by refusing to *"get out of their own way."* I'm convinced there are people who need things to complain about. It seems like they come into a room, or *wake up* complaining, or upset about something. They have a hairpin trigger, will fly off the handle at the slightest provocation, and *routinely* go from zero to full-throttle in a nanosecond! Most of us know someone who blows the simplest situations out of proportion.

They're commonly known as Drama "Queens," or "Kings." I refer to them as "Drama Creators," and the term describes exactly what they do. If there is no drama present, they'll find a way to *create* it! If you listen to them describe events as they see them, hardly anything is going right. You'll wonder if they're happy with *any* portion of their life.

If they're not complaining, they're contributing to conflicts by throwing shade at other people. They take jabs at people on social media without saying the person's name, as if those who know them, or whom they're talking about, won't (or can't) figure it out. It may be something else they're focused on, but the Drama Creator will highlight any situation, as long as it takes the spotlight off of them.

I have another philosophy that helps me simplify things: People have enough *inherited* issues to deal with, without having to deal with *invented* issues, as well. If there isn't enough to deal with already, there are people who voluntarily put barriers in their own way. But, why would a person deliberately create an issue where there isn't one?

To understand this, you have to examine the Drama Creator's mindset. They're a different type of person. Their brain doesn't operate on what many people would call a "normal" wavelength. I'm not saying they're *crazy*. There just may be a slight imbalance that they're unaware of.

This imbalance is one of the reasons a Drama Creator will routinely make a mountain out of a mole hill. They get uneasy when things are running smoothly, because they've gotten used to the drama. In essence, the drama becomes their comfort zone. Wait... didn't you read *that* earlier, too?!

To maintain their comfort level, the Drama Creator subconsciously (or maybe intentionally) invents things that go wrong. This is done because in their mind they're convinced when things go wrong, they have a license (and obligation) to insert themselves into the situation to fix it. They get a feeling of significance because they believe they're accomplishing something. Again, this makes it easy to justify their behavior.

Fixing an issue makes the Drama Creator feel like they're overcoming an obstacle, which they *are* doing. The irony is, what they're actually doing is overcoming an *invented* obstacle, by fixing an *imaginary* issue generated through *circumstances* stemming from a *perception* being driven by *emotions* created in their head. Whoa... that was a mouthful! Read it again, if you need to.

The part of the equation often overlooked by the Drama Creator is once the *invented* obstacle has been overcome, the *actual* issue (which has been in place the entire time) isn't resolved, because they haven't been able to, or have refused to identify it. *"Well, what in the world did they fix?"*

The answer to this is unfortunate, because in reality, they didn't fix anything, except an issue that shouldn't (and *wouldn't*) have been there to begin with, if it weren't for what they created in their own head. So, now they're back at the drawing board. Only this time, they're at the drawing board... *mad!* Frustration and stress levels are increased, which almost always justifies some sort of extreme action. I said this would be a tough topic for some people, didn't I?

Elevated frustration and stress levels are by-products of disappointment and misfortune. They stem from everything from the actions of other people, to the circumstances we encounter. I'm targeting these disappointments, because they lend themselves to what I stated earlier about blowing situations out of proportion.

Here's another scenario to support my argument: You ask a person to complete a task for you. They accept, and you leave them to accomplish it. Upon your return, you discover they haven't completed the task yet.

Irritated by the turn of events, you immediately start going *off* about it, relieve the person of their responsibility, and start doing the task yourself. The whole time you're doing the task, you're verbalizing sentiments of displeasure. You're not screaming, but it's loud enough so anyone within an earshot can hear. Does this sound familiar? If you've ever been married, or in a long-term relationship before, I'm certain my description struck a chord!

The tirade may, or may not have been justified. It depends on a few factors. If the person had ample time to complete the task, you had every right to go off when it wasn't completed. However here's the kicker, and many people won't want to accept this: the perception of time is purely subjective! Its impact is created completely in your head. What's *ample* for one may not be *enough* for another.

In the above scenario, two possibilities need to be explored: *Is it truly the person's inability to complete the task that triggered the outburst, or could the problem possibly be your expectations?* This is why I say many people contribute greatly to raising their own stress levels. You read earlier that people prefer to key in on ideas that validate their thinking, and shows how easily a person's mind can invent issues.

Okay, you were born with common sense. Whether you choose to *use* it or not is on you. Since you were born with common sense, you wouldn't have asked the person to complete the task if you didn't think they could do it. By and large, this nullifies the *incompetency* argument. It only leaves one other possibility: your "cookie-cutter" expectations may have triggered the tirade.

People aren't stupid. Correction – *most* people aren't stupid. As people mature, they learn to do things, and most people are intelligent enough not to accept a task they have no idea how to do, or feel unqualified to do. Therefore, it may not be their inability to accomplish the task. They may just not be accomplishing it *your* way.

Before condemning the person for not completing the task, did you ask them if they would be able to complete it within a time limit? Did you *verbalize* the time limit you had in your head *prior* to them accepting responsibility for completing the task? Finally, did they *agree* to the time limit?

In the above scenario, none of this occurred. The expectations weren't clear, which means there could have been a miscommunication between you and the other person. Had the expectations been clearly defined (including the time constraints), the person would have given you an accurate reply as to whether they could fulfill your request. Stress would have remained low, and life would have moved along without a derailment from an invented issue.

Instead, *you* decided to return when you did. When the task wasn't completed in a time limit the person *didn't know existed*, and things didn't conform to the ideal scenario you'd envisioned, an emotional spike in your head created an issue.

What followed was an outburst fueled purely by emotions, where theoretically, you focused on a negative aspect, and punished the person for not being able to *read your mind!* It sounds *terrible* when it's put that way, doesn't it?!

The outburst wasn't an unidentifiable variable. It was pretty apparent. The subtle, but more important factor is the *reason* for the outburst. As explained earlier, many people focus on the action while mostly ignoring the reason for the action, because action easily influences emotions. In this case, the tirade was emotionally-charged. I'm taking some time to discuss these *small* things that seem to have *enormous* impact.

Emotions are relatively small, compared to say, The Grand Canyon, but the power they possess could probably fill it! Emotions make people feel, whether the feeling is happiness, sadness, anger, fear, or any other you can think of. They can shift the tide of a situation in an instant. To ensure you're consistently making rational decisions, emotions must be understood and controlled as much as possible.

In my opinion, emotions contribute to the majority of the chaos we experience. More turmoil has resulted from runaway emotions than any other entity. Most of it can be traced to an emotionally-triggered reaction to a situation.

Let's put this in perspective. Normally, during a rational conversation with another person, you're listening to point/counterpoint, then, decide to agree or disagree. The moment emotions start dominating the conversation, you're no longer listening to "point/counterpoint." You're pushing *your* point! If you feel your point isn't being acknowledged or accepted, you push it harder, and most likely, *louder*. This is when communication lines break down, arguments ensue, and all the chaos associated with them follows. It's only a matter of time before resentment rears *its* ugly head.

Not many people will argue with this statement for long: *"Emotions are developed in your head."* Think about it — not one emotion is tangible! You can't hear, see, smell, taste or touch any of them. You certainly *feel* them, but exactly how much you feel them is up to you. Why would I say this?

A person's reaction is primarily due to something I call *emotional weight*. This is the amount of feeling a person assigns to a particular situation, and usually dictates the magnitude of their reaction. A massive amount of emotional weight usually triggers a massive reaction. A smaller amount of emotional weight usually triggers a smaller reaction.

The best (and worst) thing about emotional weight is the supply of it is *unlimited!* You can assign as much or as little as you want, for as long or as short of a time as you want. Need more? *Have at it…* the reserve tank is always full! What this means is, the amount of emotional weight assigned is controlled by you, and can fluctuate up or down, at *any* time.

This revelation showed me, emotions need to be kept at bay as much as possible when discussing issues, or making decisions. It wasn't easy learning how to do this, and it surely wasn't an overnight process. I don't expect you to grasp it overnight, either. It takes practice, and a lot of it. The good news is once you understand how emotions can impact decision-making, your approach to resolving issues changes.

Emotions get people into trouble because most of the time, a person is oblivious to their presence, until they're overwhelmed by them. Many people have been subliminally programmed to react to the impact of an emotion, rather than to the circumstances as they're presented. It's because emotions are nature's amplifiers. They make things appear larger than they are, which will affect your perception. Don't *believe* me? Examine the following scenario…

Someone tosses a balled-up piece of paper at you. Normally, this isn't a big deal. When you notice the paper coming toward you, what is the most likely reaction? If you function like most people, you'd probably swat it away without a second thought. After all, it's a piece of paper.

Now, run the scenario a second time. This time, instead of paper, substitute a *bowling ball*. Chances are your reaction *won't* be the same! Why? It's because of the amount of emotional weight you assign to the task of stopping an object from hitting you. You've imagined the damage a bowling ball would do if it hit you. As such, your reaction is vastly different than if it were a paper ball coming in your direction.

What you're about to read may sound odd: *"The same swatting motion used for the paper can be used for the bowling ball!"* I know — *fix your face* and try to follow my logic. It takes more *force* to swat the bowling ball, but from a physics standpoint, the swatting action can be used for either object. I'll bet many people weren't expecting that explanation!

Of course, I'd expect you to move out of the way of a bowling ball instead of trying to swat it away. That's common sense. If you *didn't* move, and actually tried to swat the bowling ball, I'd think something was wrong with you!

My "scientifically-backed" explanation is why I prefer addressing issues as they're presented, rather than relying on perception. A perception can be flawed. Dealing with issues as they're presented permits rational decisions based on facts, which ultimately lead to effective resolutions to these issues.

Conversely, if you choose to deal with the emotional aspect (as many people do), a decidedly different approach is taken. You'll tackle the emotion, because it's the immediate need, most likely with an extreme action. Do yourself a favor and learn not to deal in extremes. If an action is perceived as extreme, the counter-action will most likely *also* be extreme.

I don't want any misinterpretation of what I'm saying. I'm not referring to the occasional getting pissed off. We all get upset from time to time. I'm referring to an established *pattern* of behavior. What behavior do you display most frequently? If your pattern is reacting with extreme action, you leave the people on the *receiving* end no alternative, but to respond with their *own* extreme action. Don't know what your pattern is, or unsure if you have one? Take the suggestion from chapter 2. That person you trust will *let you know*.

Basing your actions and behavior on *possibility* will make you react differently than basing them on *probability*. For example, there's a possibility of you being robbed while walking down the street. However, walking down the street looking at every person you pass as if *they* are going to rob you will make you look *foolish!* Of course, walking down the street with $100 bills pinned to your clothes would *increase* that probability, and *would* coincide with the "reacting to possibility" mentality, but would a sensible person *do* that?!

We have society's desire for instant gratification to thank for this. We want unanticipated or unwanted emotions to subside, and we want them to subside, *right now!* To make things more challenging, as the amount of emotion-triggering items piled onto a single occurrence or statement increases, so does the amount of emotional weight levied in response. Following is an example of how something as simple as *music* can make emotional weight feel heavier than it is.

Let's compare two genres of music: old-school blues, and old-school country. Lyrically, both basically follow the same pattern. The songs are full of sad-sounding situations that can cause emotional weight to get piled on. Why? The songwriter is aiming for a desired reaction from the listener.

"My woman left me" normally doesn't trigger much of an emotional reaction. I mean, you feel for the person, but it isn't earth-shattering, because this happens quite frequently. The songwriter knows this won't trigger the reaction they're seeking, so they dig deeper into the repertoire. They employ a technique I call *stacking*, where they pile on the issues.

"My woman left me" won't get the job done, but let's read the story again, using stacking: *"My woman left me for my best friend. She took the kids and the car. My dog ran away, I lost my job, somebody stole my truck, and the house burned down!"* Hearing something like *that* triggers a much different response! You just want to do everything you can to take the pain away.

You can rest assured, this action was intentional. If you're providing a big emotional reaction upon hearing the lyrics, it's "mission accomplished" for the songwriter. They want listeners to feel. This practice works nearly every time, and *because* it's worked so well, the songs keep coming. There's nothing wrong with the practice, but listeners need to be able to differentiate reality from entertainment. If they can't (or don't), the entertainment value is mutated, and the lyrics become reality in the listener's head.

Okay, it's time to expose a secret. Well, it's not really a secret. It may have some people shifting in their seat however, because the people exposed (whom I'll call *perpetrators*) don't want other people (whom I'll call *receivers*) to know about it. I'm bringing a number of the perpetrator's tactics to the surface, to make it easier for the receivers to recognize, or be able to counter them.

For the perpetrator, this serves as a warning. Receivers are about to be educated on how you operate. If your plan is to continue trying to control receivers, you'll need to head back to the drawing board and develop a more effective strategy, because I'm about to completely *dismantle* your current one! In other words, what you currently do is about to be *"put on full-blast,"* and *"stripped down to buck-naked!"*

For the receiver, you're about to get a gift intended to help you expose some potentially damaging issues. You'll be reading important tips on how to identify, and develop countermeasures for two major issues in particular – the perpetrator, and their agenda.

75

The perpetrator is the person who wants to advance an idea they have. For whatever reason, they believe what they have to say, or what they can do, will influence others to follow their lead. To facilitate this, the perpetrator constructs an agenda, and portrays the message of that agenda as beneficial to others. This is the perpetrator's *modus operandi*. Sadly, often the agenda is only to benefit the perpetrator.

Similar to songwriters, perpetrators also rely on emotional reactions. They're crucial to an agenda's survival, because the perpetrator knows two important things: a receiver will take immediate and extreme action, to suppress any unanticipated emotions. Secondly, the more people that agree with an agenda, the further the agenda advances.

The perpetrator's success is contingent on these things occurring, but as you read in the first chapter, getting *everyone* to agree isn't their ultimate intent. They're only looking for *one* person to agree. Then, it becomes a matter of ensuring the cycle repeats. The perpetrator convinces one receiver, the receiver convinces another receiver, that receiver convinces someone else, and so forth. After so many repetitions, the agenda picks up steam and keeps on rolling.

If this cycle stops, the agenda stalls and possibly dies. To prevent this, the perpetrator presents the agenda in an over-the-top fashion, filled with sensational, often *outrageous* claims. They spout off a bunch of rhetoric designed to do nothing but stir the ire of the masses. It doesn't matter how far-fetched the idea or philosophy is, or even if it's *factual*. As long as others agree with it, the agenda's goal is being met.

This is how and why many perpetrators and receivers run into issues. The perpetrator doesn't know how, or when to stop doing what they're doing. The receiver doesn't know how to, or refuses to recognize certain things as they occur. Both become stuck in their ruts, instead of getting better.

I've read articles about some outrageous agendas. After learning about many of them I've wondered, *"How in the world did a person convince anybody to agree with this nonsense?"* It raised my curiosity and as I started doing my homework, it became easy to explain, once I understood how the chain of events unfolded. I'll share a few of those discoveries with you.

A perpetrator trying to advance an agenda *always* follows a specific formula. Even if they don't realize, or want to *admit* they're doing it… they *are!* The formula remains the same, regardless of the perpetrator, the agenda, or the reason behind it. Fortunately for the perpetrator, but *un*fortunately for the receiver – the formula *works!* It has worked for ages, and sadly, will *continue* to work as long as receivers allow their emotions to be the driving force in their decision-making.

The formula is simple, but extremely powerful: *"Say it loud, often, and with confidence."* Why is it so powerful? When employed correctly, the results of this formula are welcomed in the receiver's head, because of their perception of the idea presented. Many receivers forgo doing their own research. Instead, they assume the perpetrator has done *theirs*, and it has resulted in accurate information. You read that in an earlier chapter, in case you forgot. The only thing needed at this point, is for whatever comes out of the perpetrator's mouth to sound *reasonable*. If the receiver believes it does, they'll most likely agree with, and accept it.

This is how political candidates gain support for their campaigns. It's also how pimps coax people into prostitution. I'm not equating *all* politicians to pimps, but a comparison reveals an uncanny resemblance. Both speak very smoothly, at a rapid pace, and most of the time, in circles. Generally, a pimp speaks *much* faster than a politician, and almost *always* in circles, but the goal is the same: *gain the receiver's acceptance.*

How does this happen? The perpetrator assumes the role of manipulator. They need the receiver to see something that isn't there, but *how?* They design a pitch that appeals to the receiver's emotions. They tell the receiver what they think they want to hear, and make it sound reasonable and beneficial. The next thing you know, the unsuspecting victim willingly sides with the perpetrator. In some cases, they'll *defend* the perpetrator when confronted by an independent entity. All of this is caused by those things called *emotions.*

To illustrate how destructive uncontrolled emotions can be, I'll summarize the story of a "religious" (term used *very* loosely) group. I've read a lot of information on the group, and from what I've read, I can't exactly call what they achieved *success*. I don't know if I would call them *religious*, either! In fact, their story is stranger than fiction, but provides an excellent depiction of something I alluded to earlier: *perpetrators feast on uncontrolled emotions, to advance their agenda.*

I won't identify the group by name, because it isn't necessary. The group's name isn't as important as uncovering the level of manipulation exhibited by its leader. His actions and behavior ultimately convinced his followers to commit unimaginable acts. This one is a real head-scratcher.

The group's leader began by telling anyone who would listen to him, that he was an extra-terrestrial being, *"borrowing"* a human body to use as a transport while residing on Earth. He claimed to have come into his body, which he referred to as his "vehicle," during the 1970s. It's important to note that this man was in his late-40s when he started saying this.

His basic message was human life on Earth was about to be wiped out. According to him, the planet was about to be cleansed and recycled. The only way to survive the recycle was by leaving earth entirely, then returning at a later date.

Group members were taught (and believed) their soul would be transferred from their "vehicle" and evacuated from Earth for the duration of the recycle. A spacecraft was supposed to descend to the Earth, pick up the members, transfer their souls from their "vehicles," and transport them to an "evolutionary destination." I wish I was making this up!

The people who bought into this theory were instructed to relinquish all of their humanity-associated possessions, and were isolated from their families and friends. Outlandish as this story sounds, a number of people accepted it. The group even purchased an alien abduction insurance policy!

Maybe it's just the way my brain is wired, but I wonder who was named beneficiary, if all the people who believed this rhetoric were supposed to be leaving earth? Secondly, how would the beneficiary prove the group was actually abducted by aliens, in order to collect on the policy?

The group resided in a mansion (yes, I said mansion) and operated a computer business. While this was going on, members were told to prepare for their "exit." The group's leader instructed followers to record video messages chronicling their anticipation and excitement for their exits.

The story took a dark turn when the leader became convinced he'd received "the sign" of the spacecraft's descent in something he saw in the sky. This turned out to be a natural occurrence in space, but following his "revelation," he instructed followers to prepare for transport. They purchased identical outfits, so the spacecraft could easily identify them.

Over the next few days, the members ingested a lethal concoction, and placed plastic bags over their heads. They covered themselves with cloths and waited for the spacecraft to arrive; a spacecraft which of course, never came.

As it turns out, the video messages were nothing more than suicide notes. What struck me as strange was the person who recorded the messages. I'm not sure I could've operated a camera while listening to person after person rejoice about and anticipate their death. My mistake… I meant *exit*.

If this story isn't weird enough, the group's leader *wasn't* the last to make his "exit." Two other members assisted him. In the days following, but more importantly, after seeing *none* of what the leader said would occur, actually occur, they inexplicably *still* proceeded with ending their own lives!

Hold on... there's more! There were other members who didn't perish with the initial group, for whatever reason. Two of them carried out a suicide pact a few months later. A 3rd guy came to the mansion in the early days following the deed. He'd received a videotape of the group's plans. Once he'd verified the incident, he called authorities, but didn't tell them about the videotape until a few years later.

To cap this insane story off, the guy still subscribes to the group's principle teachings, despite over two decades of overwhelming evidence contradicting them, and history emphatically debunking the leader's theory. That is called having a lasting impact! It's worth noting that the guy *hasn't* killed himself yet, so he may not be as deranged as he sounds.

To the person of average intelligence, this story sounds *crazy as hell!* To me, it sounded like a 1950s science-fiction movie, but goes a long way to show that manipulation can be extremely tough for a receiver to recognize, and even tougher to recover from, once they've been overwhelmed by it. This is why it's important to learn about it, *before* it occurs.

The group's leader was obviously delusional, and that's putting it nicely. What he *did* succeed at, is following the agenda advancement formula *perfectly*. He had a message and delivered it with such confidence, that nearly 40 people found it reasonable in their mind, agreed with it, and willingly followed him to an untimely demise. He took the gamble that the *"loud, often, and with confidence"* formula would work, and unfortunately for the majority of his followers... it *did*.

You may be asking, *"How could anyone in their right mind believe this nonsense was reasonable?"* The only answer I've come up with is the followers *weren't* in their right mind! If they had been, they would have seen this for what it was: manipulation orchestrated by a mentally unstable person. They would have recognized the un-believability of what they were being told.

The more research I conducted on the group, the more intrigued I became. Not by the message, because I wouldn't have believed *that* for a second. I was more intrigued by the followers' thought processes, and what ultimately convinced them to *believe* what this guy was saying.

As terrible as this tragedy was, I believe the group's members shared a common characteristic: they all felt they had a void they needed to fill. Along comes *this* guy with the right message at the right moment, delivered with the right method, and a high level of confidence. The combination of these factors was enough to convince followers that his message would fill that void. Thanks to them providing the reaction he anticipated, his bizarrely-twisted agenda advanced. Whether he achieved his goal or not may never be known.

It should be easy to conclude that the group's followers operated with their emotions as the dominant force. This made it easier for them to accept the message of this clearly disturbed man. A low level of self-esteem coupled with a high level of trust in the wrong person led to their demise. The situation was caused by an imbalance in their head.

I find it appalling that nearly all the people who decided to follow this warped doctrine lost their lives over nonsense.

They were innocent victims. Looking at so-called religious groups that have suffered a similar fate, it shouldn't be difficult to see how the perpetrator's formula was executed.

This scenario played out like a made-for-TV movie, but depicts agenda advancement perfectly: Perpetrator meets receiver and recognizes low self-worth. This activates the manipulator persona. The perpetrator tells a story, or provides information that sounds reasonable to the receiver, gambling on receiving the large emotional response. If the receiver provides it and accepts, they have an instant follower!

Emotions are the gateway to manipulation if you aren't mindful of their presence. You can end up doing things you wouldn't, under normal circumstances. You must be able to recognize the signs of manipulation, because as you've seen, some people are out to serve their *own* interests, not yours.

Three factors are essential to the manipulator's success: *isolation, chaos,* and *emotional reactions.* They need the receiver to be far removed from things they're familiar with. They'll intentionally create chaos to serve as a distraction, and bank on getting emotional reactions. This leads to the manipulator being viewed as a credible source of reason. If these factors persist, the agenda advances, regardless of its validity.

When you hear a statement, keep in mind, it may or may not be factual. I'm not saying be leery of everything you hear, but consider the source, and assess what you've been told, before you react. Do this enough, and you'll get better at identifying manipulation and agenda advancement attempts. You have to beat the perpetrator at *their* game!

To curb the emotional reactions, you must break the cycle of letting your emotions run the show. If you want to reduce stress in your life, you must acknowledge that emotions can cloud your judgment, then, build formidable defenses against them. It's also a good idea to look for several tell-tale signs of a perpetrator trying to advance their agenda.

If a person is stacking bad circumstances on top of each other when they're talking to you, there's a purpose behind their action. They're trying to coax an emotional reaction out of you. They hope the more things they stack, the bigger your reaction will be. Unfortunately for many receivers, they've responded exactly as anticipated, and this has spelled success for many perpetrators. So, how does a person combat this?

Be on high alert if you notice that a person is talking *at* you, instead of *to* you. Listen for the overuse of sweeping generalizations in an attempt to quantify their claim, or if they're doing most of the talking. They don't want challenges to their rhetoric, and are trying to sound educated about the things they say, so they aren't questioned. But keep *this* in mind: an educated *fool* can cause a multitude of damage!

A perpetrator will use an abundance of adjectives and adverbs when they're speaking. Words like *"rapidly," "thousands," "millions,"* and *"disastrous"* are prime examples. Why do they do this? Perpetrators know words like these pack a powerful punch, due to their definitive connotations. They can manipulate a receiver's mindset when they're combined with a distorted perception. As a result, a topic can instantly turn emotional.

Even simple words can trigger an enormous emotional downpour, depending on how much emotional weight is assigned to them. For example, describing something as *big* will get a generally common reaction. Add the word *extremely*, and you'll get multiple different reactions. Think back to the paper ball/bowling ball scenario earlier in the chapter.

Pop quiz time! Did you catch the word *enormous* in the last paragraph? I deliberately wrote it to show how simple it is to slip words into a statement, altering your perception. This is the nucleus of the perpetrator's operation. It sounds awfully similar to how many political candidates, conspiracy theorists, and idealistic extremists communicate, doesn't it?

Emotions can make people do some strange things, like stacking things up on themselves. What's interesting about this is the things they stack may have absolutely *nothing* to do with each other! The dirty laundry they're having a hissy-fit about today, was *undoubtedly* caused when they hurt their wrist, slipping on a banana peel six years ago. That may sound silly, but there are people who display this type of behavior.

High-running emotions promote panic. When you're panicked (because of needless stacking), and can't resolve the issues you're panicked about, stress increases and leads to *more* panic. To improve, this cycle too must stop. Perpetrators and manipulators have *zero* power, until a receiver allows it!

I didn't learn this overnight. It was a process full of trial and error, and I fell flat on my face, many times. However, it wasn't until I got fed up with panicking, and decided enough was enough, that I found ways to deal with issues without allowing emotion to outweigh reason. That's when things began to shift. Emotions no longer dictate my actions, and I don't hide behind them. They certainly play a supporting role, but they aren't the lead character in my decision-making.

You must be careful when learning to subdue your emotions. If the person you're discussing an issue with has allowed their emotions to dominate, and you don't reciprocate *their* level of emotion about the issue, it can initiate a firestorm! They'll start doing things like hurling insults at you, accusing you of not caring, or even ceasing to interact with you. Some will *really* try to be slick, and accuse you of doing things *they* actually do, but conveniently leave *that* part out! Is there a clearer definition of the word *deflection?*

This of course is faulty thinking on their part that stems from a perception created *where?* In... their... head! You care as much, if not *more* about resolving the issue, but since their emotions are running rampant, they won't see that.

The reality is once you learn to deal with issues on the surface, and stop looking for emotional aspects that may (or may not) be hidden beneath the surface, you'll be focused on actual issues instead invented issues, and metaphorically *"kicking the can down the street."* You can kick the can as long as you like, but at some point, you're going to *have* to pick it up. Why not begin the cleanup, today?

Several adjustments will immediately reduce your stress level. If the stress level is reduced, you'll be more receptive to information that can help you, because you're not bombarded by things which once examined, are pretty petty.

Don't be so quick to jump into a situation. This can be a tough task if you've been "forced" to shoulder a lot of responsibility in your life. If you have, you probably feel you need to be in control, for things to be done correctly. Notice I put the word *forced* in quotations. I did that because the forcing may not be coming from others. It may be coming from *you!* You may not need to take on as much, and your assistance may not be as necessary as you think. I'll explain.

For the most part, you fill your inner circle with like-minded people. If you're intelligent, you don't normally gravitate to dumb people to associate with. You look for people who *complement* you, not people *dependent* on you.

People are capable of doing many things. You shouldn't feel you have to do everything, all the time. Don't want to cook? *Don't cook!* Don't want to clean? *Don't clean!* The world isn't going to end! If the house isn't going to burn down because the task isn't done, then it's a *want...* not a *need.*

You're *not* Superman or Superwoman, so stop trying to *"save the day!"* The amazing thing is... you *know* you're not Superman or Superwoman, yet it doesn't stop you from *trying* to be. Does that mean sit back and let someone else do *all* of the heavy lifting, as you watch them struggle? That's not what I'm saying. I'm saying learn to relinquish some control, and *trust the people in your circle.* You're around them regularly, so you know what they are, and aren't capable of. If you didn't believe they could do things without your assistance, they wouldn't be in your circle. You may not want to believe this, but many situations do *not* require your intervention.

You don't need to be in the know about *every* situation during a given day. Are you regularly involving yourself in situations between people in another room, or even another *location*? I'll reiterate: people contribute to their own stress by prematurely reacting when it's not *necessary!*

Give your brain a break! If you have a *habit* of trying to save the day, or exaggerating "normal" situations, people will start to rebel, exclude, or limit their communication with you. Why? They'll feel you'll try to *"fix something that ain't broke."* This also goes back to chapter 2: how others see *you*. Allow people to do what they do *before* chiming in, and you might be surprised by them completing the task extremely well, because they've always been able to do it. Then, *you'll* realize you've wasted a lot of time – making much ado about *nothing!*

Many people will want to debate the next statement, but logically speaking, it makes perfect sense: The direction and tone of a situation is dictated *solely* by your approach – *not* by the reactions you get. Reactions are merely secondary impulses offered in response to an initial action.

People are naturally reactive. If you initiate a situation, your role needs to be *proactive*. This means if you approach someone in a hostile manner, you have to reasonably expect a hostile reaction. What else could you expect? When people feel attacked, they're going to defend themselves.

On the flip side, approach them calmly, and nine times out of ten, you can reasonably expect a calm reaction. Can you imagine the progress society would achieve, if everyone mastered the "emotions in check" approach?

Do you notice people acting one way when they're interacting amongst themselves, but seem to be altering their demeanor when *you* come around? You think that's by chance? *Not even close!* Consider this: the situation was probably calm before you interjected, because people rarely argue amongst themselves. So… is it *them*, or *could* it be *you?*

It's plausible that your approach caused the disruption, and a 3-second shift in your thinking could have *prevented* it. You could've decided to not let the situation bother you, then, not let it bother you. Every scenario isn't, and *can't* be about you, so stop trying to *make* it about you!

Resist the urge to judge another person's performance by *your* standards. Stop expecting *you* from other people! They may not do things the way you do them, react the way you do, think the way you do, or do the things you do. You read something earlier about there being more than one method of accomplishing a task, right? If *what* you want done is *getting* done, why are you worried about *how* or *when* it gets done?

I'll *tell* you why. Going nuclear when someone doesn't share, or agree with your level of excitement or enthusiasm about a situation boils down to your need to be in control. *Surprise…* you might be a control freak! Here's a news flash: *Everyone doesn't have to panic because you panic!* People don't have to like or dislike something just because *you* do.

When you display this behavior, what you're really trying to do is control the task, as *well* as the process! *Stop it…* because you can't do both! This lends itself to prematurely reacting, and trying to change something that can't be changed. You have *zero* control over another person's actions or reactions. You only control your own.

This was a tough lesson I learned as a young supervisor. I was driving myself insane because I felt the team members weren't performing up to standards. I'd made improvement suggestions, but performances remained low. I thought, *"I can do it. Why can't they?"* It really got under my skin.

One of the best mentors I had saw my frustration and explained it, perfectly. Incompetency wasn't the problem — my *expectations* were! My tirades occurred because I measured their performances by how I would accomplish the tasks, if I had to do them. I wanted control of the task and process!

"They're not you!" he said. It took me a second to process that, but it unveiled a real problem. What I saw as important, was not as important to the team. They were unaware of my personal standards. When they failed to meet standards they didn't even know existed, I got upset. I was unnecessarily stressing because of my own flawed perception.

From that conversation, I realized shifting my mindset would benefit both the team *and* me. Firm standards and clear expectations were established and agreed to, and over the next few months, the team went from #20 to #5, and eventually was #1 in back-to-back years — a *complete* reversal!

So... is the glass half-empty or half-full? The answer depends on what I've been highlighting: your perception. The question is, "Why waste time debating?" *Drink it*, and be a problem solver! You'll *end* the debate, and *eliminate* the issue!

6. Haters... and How to Deal with Them

Thus far, you've read information about several topics that may be posing as barriers between you, and success and happiness. I've made the argument that nearly *all* of them have been created in your head, but this chapter is a bit different. I'm switching gears to examine something that can actually be created in someone else's head.

Take a moment and think about some of the people you deal with regularly. You're probably wondering, *"If this book is designed to help me, why is he asking me to consider other people?"* Good question. It's because other people are just as important to your success as *you* are. That's not to imply your success is determined solely by other people. It's determined by a combination of the support you receive from others, and your responsive actions based on that support.

The topic of this chapter has become too familiar, to far too many people. Hate is one of the biggest menaces to societal harmony. The issues associated with it, and the people who choose to display it will tear at the integrity of a community, if it isn't exposed and handled accordingly.

Our society is full of haters! If you find that hard to believe, just observe some people's behavior from time to time. Haters come in the form of family, friends, and foes, but in some cases, the hater may be a complete stranger.

If you're doing well, or what is *perceived* as doing well, you've likely had to deal with a hater. If you're fortunate, there's only been one. Depending on the level of success, some people have been forced to deal with multiple haters.

Exposing a hater can be a daunting task, because hatred isn't always blatantly displayed, but once you *can* identify them, it's an eye-opening experience! The purpose of this chapter is to snuff out the hater by providing you with enough information to help you figure out who the hater is, what they do, and most importantly... *why* they do it!

If this chapter accomplishes what I've intended, you'll have no trouble identifying a hater, as well as uncovering several effective methods of successfully engaging with them. This way, they can't derail you any more than they already have. A hater will wreak havoc on your psyche if you aren't properly equipped to handle them, but I've got you covered.

I've stated several times that you need to be prepared for the unexpected. My depiction of the hater might describe *you!* That's right... *you* might be the hater causing turmoil in someone's life! It isn't out of the question, and don't forget, we're exposing ugly truths, so you can get on track, if needed.

To get you focused, here are some basics on the hater: They hate your style of dress, how, or where you choose to live. They hate your beliefs, where, how, and whom you choose to worship, the job you have, how much money you make or don't make, or the kind of car you drive. They hate who you're in a relationship with, or other actions you take in your life. One of the easiest, yet silliest reasons a hater hates, is a person's ethnicity or nationality, as if the way a person is *born* equates to some sort of advantage, or disadvantage.

Haters can hate for a variety of reasons, and it's usually easier to handle when it's aimed at someone else, because you aren't directly affected. When the hate strikes closer to home, it alters your thinking; then, you have skin in the game.

To understand the hater's behavior, you must delve into their mind. There are things going on in there they may, or may not be aware of. *You* however, will be fully aware when you're finished reading this chapter. A hater will suck the life out of you if you let them, and that would be perfectly okay with them. But it should not, and *cannot* be okay with *you!*

Would you know if there was a hater in your life? Many people would answer yes, but could they identify *all* of them? Probably not! I say this, because haters sometimes hide in the most unlikely places, and aren't always who you'd expect.

It's reasonable to expect the hater behavior from a so-called "enemy," so it would be no surprise to find out they hate you. What *would* be surprising is uncovering a hater who has been pleasant, and regularly interacted with you! They've smiled in your face, asked how your family was doing, and if there was anything they could do for you, but behind your back, they've talked about you like you have two tails.

See if anyone you know fits this description: When you're feeling good and want to celebrate an accomplishment, someone chimes in with negativity. They do everything they can to downplay your accomplishment with their words, actions, or a combination of both. They use belittling or diminishing words and phrases like, "just," "only," and "is that it?" in their efforts to minimize what you've done.

No matter what you say, do, or how well you're doing it, they're right there, to pull the rug out from under you. It's like they're obsessed with witnessing or possibly even causing your downfall, and doing everything in their power to aid in that. Can't put a finger on anyone? Keep reading. If there is a hater lurking, you'll figure out who they are... real soon.

To identify a hater, you must understand why they exist. What makes them act the way they do? What in the world could annoy a person so badly, it would motivate them to do everything they can to rip another person's character to shreds? What could possibly cause *that* much resentment?

To put this in perspective, here's a bold statement many people won't want to believe: *"99.9% of a hater's behavior has nothing to do with you, or your actions."* I'm quite certain a few jaws dropped when they read that, and *yes*, you read it correctly! Now, let me tell you why I said it.

If you recall the basics on the hater I outlined a couple of pages ago, I'll point something out you may not have considered: *none* of those things has anything to do with the alleged hater! Each one either originates from you (like your beliefs, or style of dress), or is something no one has control over (like your ethnic makeup). It's safe to conclude that a hater's behavior is heavily swayed by what's in their head, but why would these things have such an impact? The answer I uncovered was astonishing.

Generally speaking, people enjoy witnessing the figurative destruction of another person. I know it sounds rather morbid, but it's an unfortunate reality in today's society. It makes no difference if the person being hated is a so-called celebrity, or an "ordinary" person. As long as someone is in the know about another person destroying, or has destroyed themselves, they can feel okay about their own situation, when things may not necessarily be okay.

With all of the stories, gossip, and media coverage of people's bad, or dangerous behavior being reported, it appears that we can't turn our eyes and ears away. Having first-hand knowledge of another person's misfortune gives some people a sense of satisfaction. It's a way for them to be able to say, *"I knew it all along! They're no different than me."*

This is part of the reason why reality television shows are so popular. Watching other peoples' lives implode is a source of entertainment for many viewers. These shows provide an escape from reality, if only for a while. There's no need to name any of them, because I'm sure you can insert your own favorite guilty pleasure. With their popularity we must ask, what effects do the shows have on their viewers?

For people who are unsatisfied with their lives, these shows provide a depiction of people who are like them. The viewer sees other people going through the same types of struggles, and they no longer feel isolated. This creates empathy through the use of a television show by appealing to the viewer's emotions. You can best believe it was by design.

For those who are *satisfied* with their lives, these shows are reminders of what *not* to do. They see the cast members' struggles like everyone else, but perceive it much differently than the unsatisfied person. They don't want to end up in the same boat, so they avoid replicating the cast member's actions as much as possible.

For me it's much simpler, though I lean toward the latter. These shows are nothing but entertainment, which is why I haven't watched them more than a few times. From the clips I've seen, I'm reminded that my life isn't that bad.

While we generally don't want anyone to lose their life over foolishness, viewers can't help but tune in, due to the *"What's going to happen next?"* factor. The more outrageous the behavior, the bigger the audience usually is. Producers have banked on this strategy making viewers tune in. So far, it's been a successful investment because the shows keep coming.

What satisfaction can come from the slighting of another person's accomplishments or seeing someone fail? This too is a simple answer, as most of my explanations have been, but one you may find shocking. Well, for some it may be shocking. For the hater, it'll confirm what they've known all along. You might want to hang onto your hat: *people... hate... greatness!* I can imagine the faces frowned-up, right now! Don't worry – I'll provide a rational explanation.

The satisfaction a hater experiences is the result of another ideal I've developed. *"People can't stand seeing someone else become successful, if they haven't achieved at least the same level of success, first."* Some people may need to hear that again, so I'll repeat it: *"People can't stand seeing someone else become successful, if they haven't achieved at least the same level of success, first."*

If a person hasn't reached a level of *"success"* (whatever that means in their mind) they believe they should be, they don't want *anyone* to reach that level before they do. In their rooting, they unwittingly accept a degree of content (their current status), thanks to television shows, social media, and gossip columns. They see, or read information about people stumbling in their lives, and their own life appears to be okay.

The hater relishes in the thought of contributing to the misfortune of another person, even if that contribution is only in their mind. Find that hard to believe? Take a look at social media! There are tons of hate-filled comments on everything from a person's appearance, to their social status, sexual orientation, personal, religious, and political beliefs.

It doesn't matter how poorly (or well) a person is doing, there is someone who has no connection to their situation, who feels it's their duty (and right) to chime in with an ill-mannered comment, often just to be mean. When did making malicious comments about people's imperfections, or mishaps become acceptable? I must have missed the memo.

Admittedly, some of the comments are funny, but many are brutal, and downright hurtful. Reading them sometimes reminds me of something else my dad said (and I love this): *"Sometimes, it's perfectly okay and appropriate just to shut your mouth. This way, people don't get the wrong impression, and assume you're stupid. But… if you open your mouth enough times with stupid stuff coming out of it, eventually, you will confirm the assumption!"*

The point I'm making is you don't need to make a comment about everything you hear, or see. Some things are simply *not* your business! So, why keep trying to *make* it your business? I'll remind you of the Drama Creator who needs to fix invented issues, in order to maintain their comfort level. Here's something to consider: Watching from the sidelines teaches you much more, because the scope of vision is wider.

Posting information on social media opens a person up to a swarm of good and bad comments. It comes with the territory, but some people go needlessly overboard. They're spoiled by the convenience of information in cyberspace. It has resulted in desensitization to many things, and has created a powerful illusion, where people think they can say and do as they please, without consequences. They often don't take time to think about the impact their actions may have on others.

The amount of accessible content feeds the illusion. On any given day, you can find a picture, or video that has gone viral, depicting someone doing something funny, dangerous, violent, or just outright stupid. There's no need to get into specifics. I'm sure you've seen plenty.

Technological advances have given many people a false sense of security, which adds fuel to their boldness. A flawed presumption of anonymity has made many people believe what they say or do behind their computer screen can't reveal clues to their identity, and/or location. News flash, folks: if someone wants to find you... they can! A computer screen doesn't make you as anonymous as you think.

I'm an advocate of personal interaction. Regrettably, it's becoming a trend of the past. People have become more comfortable with discounting other's feelings because of the increasing impersonal environments promoted by items we use daily. Computers and smartphones only require *you* to operate them. Many popular video games are designed for one player. Tablets and personal music players don't promote much personal interaction. Online banking and ATMs make it possible to access your accounts without ever walking inside a bank. You can even buy gas *at the pump!*

Notice I said *interaction*, and not *communication?* These two should not be confused. It's possible to communicate with someone without talking to them directly, thanks to email, social media, online gaming, and the text message. While communication does occur with an email or text, it's the receiver's interpretation of what's being sent that will determine the timeliness and magnitude of their reaction. The interaction factor is omitted. Technology has certainly made our lives more convenient individually, but collectively, it's killing the art of personal interaction. As such, it's easy to become numb to another person's feelings.

What I'm doing is painting a very vivid picture of the hater. If you haven't figured out how already, you should soon have no trouble recognizing many of the hater's tactics and how they affect you. If you discover you *are* the hater, I hope you'll understand how your actions affect the atmosphere and people around you, and it prompts you to make adjustments, so you can make *your* life more enjoyable. You're only in this life for a limited amount of time. Why not make the most of your time, instead of trying to manage somebody else's? It's a much easier route to take.

In the following scenario, I'm going to pick on women for a bit. This isn't intended to be sexist in any way, so don't go getting your face all frowned up when you read it. I simply want to show how quickly a situation can go awry, and subsequently activate the hater.

A nice-looking woman walks into a hair salon she's never been to, looking to get her hair done. Ladies, I know that's a scary thought, but try to stay with me on this. The salon is full, but she doesn't recognize anyone in there. She greets the first stylist she sees. The stylist says she won't be able to get in a chair for almost another 2 hours, as there are a number of ladies in front of her. The woman can't wait that long. She politely thanks the stylist and leaves. She wouldn't get 50 feet away from the door, before a conversation similar to the following takes place:

"Oh… that heffa thinks she's cute!"

"I know, right? She thinks she's too good to wait like the rest of us?"

"I don't know who she thinks she is, walking in here like she's the Queen of Sheba! Especially with that tired-looking weave in her head!"

What?! Were they inside the woman's head? Did she walk over and specifically *say* to one of them, *"I think I'm cute?"* Because, unless she *did*, or they *were* inside her head, they have no idea *what* that lady was thinking! Lastly, did she *have* to be a "heffa?"

Situations like this are an example of how the hater is activated. Their actions are brewed from a perception or assumption, and are usually perpetuated by subsequent agreements. Something created in a person's head can trigger a chain of events. By now, you should be able to see the behavioral pattern, but I'm still not quite ready to reveal it.

This example may sound humorous, or extreme to some people, but it isn't that far-fetched. Scenarios like this take place pretty frequently in virtually every society: urban, suburban, or rural. I've witnessed situations like this first-hand, and haven't spent much time in hair salons.

If you've never witnessed anything like this, watch the movies, *Beauty Shop* or *Steel Magnolias*. The characters in these movies personify my scenario perfectly. To ensure I'm not accused of solely picking on women, you can also watch the *Barber Shop* series of movies. In them, the hater personas are partially depicted by men. So there!

By now, you should have a good understanding of who the hater is, as well as why they exist. Next is learning to recognize what they do. There's a platform the hater prefers to work from, and you need to know what it is. This can be tricky because hater tactics can take on different forms, but I'll dissect the hater's behavior, so it's no longer a mystery.

Haters have an arsenal of tactics they're extremely good at using. They've practiced them so often, and for so long, they can execute them with little effort. This is because the hater spends a massive amount of time and energy putting another person (who I'll call the *target*) down.

For whatever reason (fair or unfair), the hater doesn't like something about the target. The hater makes it their mission to ensure the target's character remains in a negative light, with anyone who will listen to them. Discrediting the target in any and every way is high on the hater's priority list.

If, or when things go wrong for the target, the hater is more than satisfied to learn about the misfortune. You can almost visualize the smile on their face. They do this because they've done something to contribute to tarnish the target's image, even if that contribution is only in their own mind.

In my opinion, the hater spends *too* much time trying to make the target look bad, and not *enough* time trying to make themselves look good. To make matters worse, the target is normally clueless to the level of the hater's contempt.

Social media is one of the hater's favorite platforms. In case you didn't know, information on social media travels fast! It doesn't matter if the information is factual or not, justified or not. It doesn't take long to circulate. A hater can say what they want without interruption, then, ignore any rebuttals or contradictions. You think I'm kidding? Do a search for "(Celebrity's name) Haters." Go ahead... I'll wait.

Everywhere you look, there's some website, blog, or group dedicated to hating a particular celebrity, person or group of people. There are hundreds, if not thousands of them. It seems like almost daily, some hater posts or says something negative about their target, but *why?* Why would someone take the time to create a forum with the specific purpose of publicly displaying hatred for another person?

Again, it just may be the way my brain is wired, but if I don't like someone, I won't be talking about them every 15 minutes. Frankly, I have better things to do. No one I dislike deserves *that* much "free rent" in my head, and I refuse to spend my time worrying about someone who has little to no bearing on my life. It boggles my mind why an adult would spend time talking to another person about their dislike for a *third* person, *unless* it isn't actually dislike. It may be *infatuation!*

The truly sad part is when a hater makes futile attempts to justify their hatred, by saying things like, *"I told you,"* or *"See... look at this?!"* There's little the target can do, to prompt the hater to give them credit for anything. The target could discover a cure for *cancer*, but all the hater would want to talk about is how big they think the target's *head* is.

Sometimes, a hater's disdain for their target is so deep-rooted (and it sounds insane), they will ignore, or argue with facts, disregard scientific evidence, reason, and logic, in order to keep their hatred intact. You remember my parents' lesson about arguing with facts, right? The hater may even resort to believing, and in some cases, making up complete *nonsense*, as long as it or someone else validates their thinking.

The clinical term for this is *confirmation bias*. It describes how a person gravitates to information that validates their beliefs, but intentionally ignores information that contradicts those beliefs. If you think about it, it's self-deception.

It isn't so unnerving that the hater hates. You can deal with that rather easily. The challenge is uncovering the reason (or reasons) for their hate and dealing with that. Once you grasp *why* the hater hates, you can educate yourself effectively on how to handle them.

Are you familiar with the expression, *"Misery loves company?"* Unless you've lived in a cave most of your life, you've likely heard it at least once. At its core, the expression rings true, but I believe there's more to it. I tend to look at things a bit differently, as I'm certain you've noticed, by now.

Misery indeed loves company, but my personal spin on this adage presents a different perspective: *"Misery needs company!"* Whoa! Think about this a minute: misery cannot thrive in a positive environment. It's impossible! Misery relies on fuel, and the only fuel for misery is *more* misery.

Imagine a nightclub: music playing, people enjoying themselves, having drinks, socializing, laughing, and dancing. In walks a person with their face frowned up, obviously in a bad mood. How many people would notice them, right away? I would, because that's my observant nature, but most people would continue enjoying themselves – completely oblivious to Mr. or Ms. Frowny Face.

It wouldn't be until their misery gained momentum, and became the dominant emotion in the room, that the tone of the atmosphere begins to shift. We discussed the influence of emotions on a person's actions in the last chapter. Here's an example of how it happens. The way the scenario unfolded ties it to the discussion of haters and their behavior.

Haters routinely exhibit certain behavior characteristics. They can't help it, and it doesn't matter who they are. The troubling thing is many people are oblivious to them. They inadvertently overlook signs that can easily reveal the hater's behavior. Usually, these signs aren't addressed until they're smacking the person in the face.

The nightclub's atmosphere didn't start shifting until Donald (or Debbie) Downer became the focus. If the momentum of a situation shifts to a direction we weren't expecting, our emotions instinctively kick in and we want the situation resolved as quickly as possible. The key is resolving the problem, not the emotion. Many people do the opposite, and end up launching an attack at the wrong target.

This is why it's important to pay attention to what a person says, but to what they do. A large portion of communication is non-verbal, so a lot of what a person is saying *isn't* coming out of their mouth. Non-verbal communication provides you with insight into the hater's mind and reveals the truth about their behavior, even if the person is lying through their teeth while they're talking to you. It may not be as easy to uncover the motives for their behavior, but it can soften the impact if you can recognize the warning signs sooner rather than later.

I have a suspicion the next few paragraphs are going to make a few people *extremely* uncomfortable. They're about to come face-to-face with some harsh realities. Hopefully, they'll remember the challenge I laid down in the first chapter.

Some people will try to argue with the following statement, though I suspect most of those arguments won't last very long: *"Hate is a wasted emotion! It does more to keep the* *hater at bay, than it does tearing the target down. Every minute you spend hating someone else, means something in your <u>own</u> life is being short-changed by that same minute!"*

When you hold onto hatred and anger, you'll find yourself regularly searching for ways to badger the target's image. While you're looking for reasons to be upset with them, your target is clueless to your behavior. So, who is the anger really affecting? Certainly not the target! A person can't be negatively affected by something, if they don't know it's exists. Therefore, the anger is only eating *you* up inside. Furthermore, unless you're getting the desired reaction from the target, your anger is being misguided.

Here's something else to chew on about holding on to anger: You're essentially relinquishing power over a portion of your life to whatever person or thing you're spending time hating! What's worse is the person or thing may not *want* the power you're giving them/it. Reading that sucked, didn't it?

This is a lesson I learned from a past relationship. For legal reasons, I won't identify the woman by name, but logically there's no reason to. Her identity isn't as important as highlighting the effect her actions had on me, and the invaluable information I gained from dealing with her.

I held a major grudge against this woman for a long period of time – like some *years!* My disdain for her was at a level I'd have to classify as *absolute* hatred. If this woman was on *fire*, and I had the only water within a thirty-mile radius, I'd *drink* it despite not being the least bit thirsty! I despised the ground she walked on, and that's as nice as I can put it.

What made me so angry with her is she knew about the emotional scars I'd suffered. I was still reeling from a divorce, and that wasn't helped by the several failed relationships that followed. Truthfully, I had no business getting into a new relationship without healing first, but I tried it, anyway!

I told her how my past relationships had devastated me. She looked at me and swore she'd never do *"anything like that."* Wouldn't you know... she ended up doing *exactly* that! So in *my* eyes, her actions weren't inadvertent. They were *deliberate*, and she had no problem doing them.

Since she had no problem with her actions, I had no problem with expressing my displeasure directly to her face! I saw no error in the manner I spoke to her, because I was blinded by hatred. It made it easy to justify my behavior, and I didn't have to provide an explanation for the way I felt. I'm thankful she only saw the surface hatred. It probably would have scared her to death if she saw the hatred I was hiding *beneath* the surface! Yes... my hatred for her ran *that* deep.

For a while, I took pleasure in trashing her image to anyone who would listen to me. I racked my brain daily, thinking of ways to make her life more miserable than she'd made mine. I thought of every sinister action I could to get back at her. My intent was ensuring she never made the mistake of screwing with me (or anyone else), again!

Not once did it occur to me that despite all my planning to destroy this woman, she went on living her life as if she didn't have a care in the world! My reaction to what she did gave her a platform to showcase her actions. I tipped my hand and showed her she could get a rise out of me. I was providing the anticipated emotional response while she enjoyed watching me make a fool of myself.

What was really happening (and it was tougher than shoe leather for me to accept), was *her* actions had more influence on the direction of my life than my *own* actions! My anger wouldn't allow me to see beyond what she'd done to me. I was spiraling out of control.

Oddly enough, although I knew it wasn't good for me to think this way, I was willing to take the ride to destruction. Why? I was convinced that revenge was what I needed for redemption. Oh, but did life have a surprise in store for *me!*

It's interesting how life takes command of a situation when you don't want it to. At the moment you think you have the upper hand, life shows you otherwise. It forced me to come to an ugly realization: I'd lost track of my life due to a preoccupation with revenge. Instead of handling the hater in *my* life, I *became* the hater in *hers!* Once that soaked in, it was a powerful wake-up call!

The "turning point" as I've termed it, came during a perfectly-timed conversation. Despite all the trash-talking I'd done about this woman behind her back as well as to her face, she agreed to meet to discuss some things. Believe me – I had more than *some* things to discuss with her!

From the outset, I let her *have it!* Every ounce of anger I had in me, came rushing out as if a flood gate had been opened. I told her (assisted by an *abundance* of colorful words) what occurred between us was jacked up. I called her every ugly name imaginable, and then, made up some *new* ones! I felt good about finally being able to give her a piece of my mind, unfiltered, and uninterrupted.

To this day, I'm amazed she didn't walk away from me. I wouldn't have blamed her if she had, because my conduct was disgraceful! If the roles were reversed, I assure you she would have been left standing there by herself, looking silly. Remarkably, though I was talking about her like a dog, she sat there and listened to my hate-filled, profanity-laced tirade.

In what now seems like the blink of an eye, an unbelievable, but significant event occurred. In the midst of my emotional meltdown, a voice in my head kept repeating, *"You'll never be able to move on with your life, until you let this anger go."* I tried to ignore it because I was on a roll, but the voice was louder than my tirade, and it wouldn't let up.

After a few minutes, I finally relented. Then just like that, in mid-sentence, my "purge" ended as abruptly as it began! Whatever opened that flood gate suddenly closed it. My entire demeanor changed, and I'd never felt such a sense of calm. What happened next is nothing short of a miracle.

Out of nowhere, I told this woman who'd dragged me through the mud, I *forgave* her. If that wasn't enough, I *apologized* to her! Not for what I said, but for the way I said it. I had no right to disrespect her in that manner.

Right then, I felt a huge weight lifted off my shoulders. I have to attribute it to *divine intervention*, because two things I knew for certain: 1) I'd reached my boiling point, and 2) I was determined to finish my tirade.

In a unique twist of fate, *her* reaction to *my* reaction absolutely floored me. This was the surprise life had for me. She accepted my apology and did something I never expected her to do. She took ownership of *her* actions, and apologized for *her* role in fueling my anger. She said she saw my viewpoint, and felt terrible about how things transpired.

I was *stunned!* I'd finally gotten the vindication I'd sought, but had no clue how to react upon receiving it. Her admission took all my ammunition away and there was nothing left for me to say. I felt the smartest thing to do was leave. So, I thanked her for listening and excused myself.

Who knows how far the situation would've escalated, had it continued? In my state of mind at the time, it probably wouldn't have ended well for me. I'm grateful for the higher forces on duty that day for intervening. They prevented me from heading down a path that because of my anger towards her, I might not have been able to recover from.

It didn't hit me until later, but at the moment I forgave her, I'd retrieved the power I'd allowed her to have over my life. That path appeared again, but this time, it looked quite different. It was now lighted and paved, with directional signs. I received the clarity I needed to start taking control of my life on *my* terms. The script had been successfully flipped!

This is the approach I suggest adopting if you want to successfully deal with a hater. You can't allow the hater to possess the lion's share of power over your life. That power should be reserved for you! If you've just discovered this is what has been happening, it's time for you to wrestle that power back. You have to shift the paradigm and ensure that power is beneficial to *you*, not the hater.

Hopefully, this is a vivid enough description of how a hater's behavior can affect you. Their actions can throw you completely off your game, and even turn *you* into a hater! I handed another person control of my life, and she had no idea of how much power she really had. My anger was the culprit, because I'd allowed it to *dictate* my behavior. There I was – willingly, but *unwittingly* performing as her puppet.

In another ironic twist, since that confrontation, our lives have taken decidedly different paths. I can say for the most part I've been satisfied with the path I've taken. She on the other hand, might need to be reading this book!

If you don't treat people fairly, it'll come back to bite you. I forgave her and left the situation alone. I didn't forgive her for *her*. I forgave her for *me*, because I value my sanity. I then had to forgive myself for feeling the way I did. That's when fate stepped in and straightened out the chaos, proving itself once again to be the "Ultimate Equalizer."

Even armed with the above information, many people will still choose (and yes, it's a *choice*!) to embrace the role of a hater. The rush a hater receives from witnessing another person's figurative demise may be indescribable, or inconceivable to others, but it makes sense in their mind.

By now, you should be able to identify the hater, as well as many of the tactics they use to exhibit their behavior. What's left is the third and most important piece of the puzzle: why they do it. When you assemble the puzzle, the hater's mentality becomes very easy to decipher.

You must understand that you may not have done anything to provoke the hater. I say this, because again, the majority of the hater's animosity is dictated by what's in their head. Something about you has prompted the hater to think, or speak unfavorably about you. Regardless of *what* they hate, their hatred *always* stems from at least one of three things.

Number 1: *the hater perceives you as a threat.* You may not have specifically expressed a threat. Well, in some cases you may have, but most times, you wouldn't know you're being perceived as a threat. But why would someone see you as a threat if you don't see yourself as one? It's because in their mind, somehow, you are threatening to their well-being. Survival instincts kick in, and they launch a counterattack to neutralize the threat. This is a primary depiction of *fear.*

The hater develops a fear of becoming insignificant — being overshadowed by *your* actions and accomplishments. Their natural recourse is to display extreme or over-the-top actions or behavior, in efforts to try to drown out what you do, and hang onto a perceived "position of power." Do I need to mention again, that all of this occurs in their head?

Number 2: *the hater wants to be you.* Any way you slice it, this is nothing but *envy!* You have something the hater wants, and it is one of these five "Ps": Person, Possession, Position,

Power, or Personality trait. You may be in a relationship with the type of person they want. You may be in a relationship with the *person they want!* Maybe you live in a neighborhood they want to live in, have the family or job they want, or drive the car they want. The list can go on, but an aspect of your life has made such an impact on the hater, they find it necessary to find (or invent) fault with you.

This is usually done because the hater is unhappy with an aspect of their life. Shifting the focus diverts their attention to you, and the issue doesn't appear to be with them. If they can find a way to conclude that you're a dirt bag, they can say, *"They just got lucky"* instead of *"They worked their butt off to get where they are."* Convincing themselves of this makes rationalizing their actions and behavior easier.

This practice is commonly seen with celebrities, who frequently have to contend with scores of haters. People see celebrities and become envious. They're going to nightclubs, parties, on luxury vacations, living in extravagant houses, etc. The hater sees this and wants what the celebrity appears to have. I say *appears*, because the hater's animosity is likely due to speculation, driven largely by perception. Unless they have regular interaction with them, the hater usually has no idea what the celebrity endures on a daily basis.

Normally, a hater's reaction when it comes to a celebrity is based on what most people have – *assumptions.* They see the celebrity in the media and assume they know them, when in reality, what they know is their public persona, which may be completely different from their personality.

What's often overlooked by the hater when judging that public persona is whether the celebrity is happy or not.

There have been numerous stories of celebrity suicides, and many of them sound eerily similar. The person appeared to live in the lap of luxury; good-looking, rich, and talented. Yet, despite the perks of a so-called "good life," these people still battled personal demons. Unfortunately, the pain caused by those demons, was dominant enough to convince them that their best option to escape the pain was ending their own life. They opted for a *permanent* solution to *temporary* problems. I think it's safe to conclude that celebrity status doesn't always equate to happiness.

Don't fool yourself into believing haters only plague celebrities. Non-celebrities encounter haters, too. Just because you don't have fame or a ton of money in the bank, doesn't mean you're immune to haters. A non-celebrity's hater can cause *more* damage. In most cases with celebrities, they don't personally know the hater, but many have found out the hard way, the closer a hater is… the bigger impact they can have.

It's disheartening to discover that a hater is a longtime friend, or even worse – a *relative*. It's unfathomable to think someone close to you would be internally rooting for your figurative demise, but it *does* occur, probably more than we'd like to think. The sting of *this* hater penetrates much deeper than if there was no personal connection to the hater. Dealing with the "internal" hater isn't always as easy as cutting them off. You can only hope with luck and over time, the hatred subsides and eventually dies out.

This brings me to the third reason the hater hates. Your existence or the things you've accomplished are a constant reminder of things they haven't accomplished in their own life. What's worse is they face them every time they see, or think about you. This is a typical characteristic of *self-hatred*.

This one is tough for the hater, because it forces them to acknowledge things they may have been ignoring. Reality punches them in the mouth, and they can no longer sweep it under the rug and pretend it doesn't exist. Watching another person actually accomplish things they've always wanted to do themselves, but still haven't is infuriating to the hater.

You might want to hang onto your seat again, because what I'm about to say may be difficult for you to believe, but logically, it makes perfect sense: You (the target) have done something quite remarkable, simply by being who you are. How is that remarkable? Well, by being who you are, you managed to *exceed the hater's expectations of you!*

The moment you exceeded the hater's expectations, you invaded a portion of their comfort zone they didn't expect you to reach, and seized control of something you were never expected to obtain. Thus, you became a threat to their comfort. They expected you to be one place, but you ended up in another. Their defensive instincts kicked in, and they're looking for that familiar feeling of comfort. This triggers some bizarre behavior that is usually propelled by *panic* or *fear*.

At this point, the hater will start looking for any and everything they can find, to try and revile, ridicule, mock, or belittle you, in efforts to tear your character down, even if that means resorting to making stuff up about you! What's worse is they'll spread it to anyone who'll listen to them.

When a hater can't control *their* image of you, they try to control *other* people's image of you. It sounds ridiculous, but to a hater, if others have a similar perception to theirs, they won't be the only person who'll look crazy for hating you, if the thing they hate about you is proven incorrect, false, or just plain stupid. For them, there's comfort and safety in numbers. This is an unnecessary power struggle that I'll reiterate again, is taking place inside the hater's head!

The hater made the incorrect decision to sell you short, and you succeeded despite their best efforts to sabotage you. In short, you *pissed them off!* You did nothing out of the ordinary, except be yourself, but this simple action impacted the hater's life so immensely, them being witness to your accomplishments forced them to reflect on their own shortcomings, and angered them. That is some serious power you probably didn't even realize you had!

How can you benefit from this? You shift these odds, by making the circumstances created by the hater work for *you!* The hater made a critical mistake, and their plan for your demise failed. It's now time for you to stop selling *yourself* short! Understand this: you have a trait in you the hater sees value in. It's important for you to find out what that trait is, because it *has* to be good! Why *else* would they hate it?

In my opinion, the hater's behavior is nothing more than a smokescreen for deeper issues. The hater doesn't want to see anyone else succeed while they remain in a rut. Hating on the target, if only temporarily, shifts their focus away from the person they see in the mirror, or think about when they're alone. Instead, the focus is on the target. This way, their rut appears non-existent, when in reality, it hasn't gone anywhere. This is a classic self-diversion tactic.

What's troubling about this third reason, is instead of developing a plan to turn things around, the hater is content with remaining within the boundaries of their comfort zone. They'd rather spend time tearing down the target's character in efforts to look good to others, or maybe just to themselves.

Here's where you have an advantage. The hater has a problem with *your* existence – it isn't the other way around! You have no choice but to accept your existence. To you, you are who you are, but to the hater, you are who they *think* you are! You are their perception of you, which is created *where?*

What will make the difference for you when dealing with a hater is *your* perception of the *hater!* A hater isn't a huge negative burden once you understand their behavior. As bad as the effects of a hater can be, they can also be a catalyst. You can use the hater's disdain as a source of strength for you, like they use your existence as a source of anger for them. The reality is the hater sees something *extremely powerful in you!* You need to see it, too!

A trait in you is shining so prominently, the hater uses it to justify contempt towards you. Figure out what they see. If it's good, keep doing it. If it's not, *stop* doing it. Remember, your legacy is determined by your actions that make the biggest impact. What traits are your actions exhibiting?

You must use the hater's behavior as fuel. If they think the trait would be beneficial to them, why can't it be beneficial to you, instead? If the trait is detrimental, you only need to alter your behavior. Make the situation work to your advantage, and you can *really* give the hater something to hate!

Good, bad, or indifferent, if the hater didn't recognize the potential impact of that powerful trait you have, they wouldn't be spending their time and energy trying to *suppress* it! People only suppress what they feel will cause damage if it were allowed to develop. Fire *suppression*, voter *suppression*, and emotional *suppression* are a few examples. Fire, voters, and emotions – each of these can cause significant damage, if allowed to grow or develop. If the hater is fearful of this damage, they'll spare no expense on damage control.

There is a downside to effectively applying this newly-acquired knowledge. Becoming successful despite a hater's attempts to derail you will most likely make them despise you even more, until they're ready to alter their behavior. It'll drive them absolutely insane when they realize their sabotage attempts have no effect on you. However, you'll be too busy improving your life to notice, or even *care*.

In a weird way, it might be appropriate to thank the hater. I know it sounds strange, but at the same time, makes perfect sense. You don't have to thank them directly, but somewhere inside of you, appreciate what they've done for you. Thanks to their behavior, you're reading this chapter, which has given you a lot of information you need to identify them, know why they exist, and know the tactics they use.

It's also given you three rational-sounding explanations for why the hater does what they do. The key for you now is forming a counter-action strategy. The hater has had a degree of power over you, because you've allowed them to have it. It's time for you (like I did) to retrieve that power.

Retrieving power sounds like a frightening task, but I assure you, it isn't as hard as you may think. Why am I so sure about that? The truth is you've always *had* the power, at least in one person's mind – the hater's. It's high time you recognized it in *your* mind. Sometimes all it takes is a small, but key piece of information to get things moving. Remember this: an avalanche can start out as a snowball.

Two more important points I want to make about haters. If you can burn these into your memory, it'll make dealing with a hater a snap. First point: haters don't hate *"just because."* They hate because they see something in *you* that makes *them* uncomfortable! Either they don't have the "something," and seeing you display it (whatever it is) is driving them absolutely nuts. Or if they have it, they're refusing to acknowledge it. To maintain their comfort level, they must tear down the target. If they can accomplish this, they can then feel comfortable around the target.

Secondly, people won't waste their time hating something they see as *insignificant* or *invaluable*. If you're now able to identify a hater, you need to realize that they chose to direct their hate toward you because something about you (at least in their eyes) is either significant, valuable, or *both*, and it's being perceived as threatening to their comfort.

119

Based on this information, what's your next move? If you want to keep your sanity, it'd better be finding a way to alter the motion of the pendulum. It's time to close the current chapter, and begin a new one with *you* as the main character. You are in control of how your story unfolds.

Don't fool yourself into thinking you're going to stop someone from hating you. You're not. There are people who have it in their heart and mind to hate. You can't change a person's mind or heart, so don't waste your time trying. They must want to change it themselves. Don't forget, the hater has the issue – not *you!*

For those sitting dumbfounded with your jaw on the ground, or your lip poked out because you just discovered that *you* are the hater, not to worry! Your situation isn't lost. There is help and hope for you, and the turnaround begins in your head.

Many newly-identified haters won't want to accept this, but I'll say it, anyway: *"You don't hate your target!"* Yes, you read that correctly. You don't actually hate your target. What you hate is *your thought* of your target! Your resentment stems from a perception, which you already know is developed in your head. So, what you've really been doing is wasting your time hating something *imaginary!* Go ahead and chew on *that.*

How can you reverse the effects of this action? Consider the suggestions I gave your target, and take back control of your life. Instead of wasting time and energy hating your target, spend your time and energy working on the person *you* are! In other words… *mind your own business!*

I want to make sure something is crystal clear: It's *never* okay to hate someone! However, if you must, make sure you're hating them for their actions against you *directly*, and not for who you *think* they are, or what you *think* they did! If you don't take this advice and continue to hate, you might be hating something that isn't really there, and yes... this will make you look and sound *crazy!*

If you choose to hate, you need to face two important facts: 1) Hate is a *learned* behavior. No one is born hating. 2) Your target will never know the true level of the hatred you have toward them. Only you know that. So, it makes more sense to make positive adjustments to your own life, and you can *stop* being the hater in someone *else's*.

It isn't your target's fault that you created issues with them based on a possibly flawed perception. They were busy living their life. The animosity you're carrying around is only preventing you from living *yours!* You have to let it go, or it will consume you. Take it from someone with experience, and keep *this* in mind: despite outward appearances, you don't know your target's struggles, or if they're happy. Laughter and smiles have shown in many cases, they can conceal a lifetime of pain, anger, depression, and unhappiness.

Perhaps the issue is deeper than you imagine. Directing hatred toward the *perceived* target might be your method of keeping it pointed away from the *actual* target... *you!* That's a chilling thought, but here's the good news: you don't have to remain that way. Shifting your mindset will go a long way toward minimizing, or even eliminating the issue.

In our society, there is more than enough opportunity for success and happiness to go around. In fact, every person can have their respective share, and there would still be plenty left over. Similar to emotional weight, the reserve tanks for success and happiness are always full. So, stop worrying about someone else's share, and go get your own! What you need to do is occupy your time with positive influences, so the negative influences don't have a chance to ruin it for you.

To shift the odds if hatred is the obstacle you're dealing with, remember it only stems from three sources: *fear, envy,* or *self-hatred* – nothing else! Additionally, *all* of these are an absolute waste of your time, if you're trying to improve your life, because you don't control anyone else's life. Keep *that* in mind the next time you decide to hate somebody.

You can *never* underestimate the power of fate! It has a nasty, effective way of settling the score. If you spent more time building yourself up, you'd likely realize you don't have much time (or room) to waste tearing someone else down.

Educator Booker T. Washington is quoted as saying, *"You can't hold a man down without staying down with him."* If you're spending a lot of time trying to discredit, or stifle someone else's progress, what message could you possibly be communicating to others about your *own* character? Are you overcompensating with the hatred, in order to conceal some insecurity, out of fear of what your target may become, and you'll be left behind, stagnating in the same position you're currently in? Here's a news flash for you: hate doesn't control anyone's destiny except *yours*. So, stop *feeding it!*

7. Relationships

Oh boy! This is the chapter I was most concerned about. Not because I was afraid to write it. I believe out of all the chapters in this book, *this* one will likely cause the most controversy, mainly due to what I mentioned earlier: people generally aren't as receptive to a contradictory point of view.

While I was brainstorming for the book, people told me I was absolutely *nuts* to take on this topic without scientific evidence to back up what I'm saying. However, I believe in simplifying concepts to get a point across. In my opinion, common scenarios people can relate to don't need science to explain them. You'll see what I mean as you read the chapter.

Let's face some facts: society's record with relationships isn't the greatest. More relationships have been dissolved than have remained intact, and it's probably for the best in many cases. But think about this: oddly enough, *every* failed relationship began as a *pleasant* one!

If a relationship has failed, somewhere along the road to "failed" it took a detour from "pleasant." If we're ever going to become better at developing healthy relationships, it's imperative to find out what makes them succeed. It also means uncovering some of the things that cause them to fail, though some of those things may not be as enjoyable to read.

Get comfortable, because this by *far* is the longest chapter in the book. I tried my best to shorten it. I knew the kinds of thoughts it would provoke, which is why I dreaded writing it. However, the more I analyzed it, the more I realized that deleting too much information from it would distort the chapter's message. So, I decided to leave it as is.

Developing an understanding of what goes right or wrong in a relationship isn't a fast, or an easy process, especially if the objective is convincing someone that they may be the *cause* of it going right or wrong. Several interesting aspects need to be explained, and that's what I'll try to do.

I expect to take some heat for this chapter's content, because a few people are about to come face-to-face with some alarming discoveries about themselves. Add emotions to that mix, and they'll get extremely agitated, particularly if they can't mount a defense, or a counter-argument to what they've read. Some of this is going to sting... and sting *hard!*

The people most affected by this probably won't want to admit it, and I can't say I blame them. Nobody wants to come to the realization that *they* are the one who's wrecking (or has wrecked) a relationship. It's much easier to assign blame than to take responsibility. I'm hoping my explanations reduce some of the heat, but I'm not betting the farm on it.

There are people who are going to read this chapter and because of their comfort zone, lean on deflection or denial as a safeguard. The internal conversation will probably sound something like, *"As long as I can point the finger at someone or something else, and say it's because of that, these bad things are happening to me, I can look in the mirror and be okay with the person staring back. I'd hate being forced to admit I'm just being stupid!"*

Ironically, learning to take responsibility for the good, and the bad experiences is part of maturing. There are times when you *are* just being stupid. The key is to own and learn from those experiences, so you don't *continue* being stupid!

Nearly everyone will agree that relationships aren't easy. I'll add something to that, but it might make it difficult for many people to accept. However, barring attempts to remain in denial, they should have no problem accepting it when they finish this chapter, because it's 100% accurate: *"Relationships aren't easy, but they aren't nearly as hard as people keep trying to make them!"* and I mean it exactly the way you read it.

I'll be highlighting a number of the behavioral actions that contribute to the success or failure of a relationship. There isn't enough time to discuss *every* reason a relationship succeeds or fails. We could discuss it for days and still not find a resolution. This topic alone could be its own book.

Here's a chapter overview. I figure if I tell you what you'll see before you see it, *when* you see it you'll have to laugh because I already told you it was coming. The chapter is divided into four sub-chapters, and mainly centered on romantic relationships, but most of the information can apply to any relationship, whether it's romantic, social, platonic, or work-related. All relationships proceed or stall, on the same premise: clear communication, or a lack thereof.

I'll be discussing women, but *purely* from my observations. I'm not inside any woman's head, and will not pretend I know how their brain works – I *don't!* Nor do I believe my depictions apply to *all* women. Obviously, they won't, but I've seen them enough to know they happen quite often. I can however, discuss men from observation and experience with no problem. I can do this because, I've been single, committed, married, estranged, *and* divorced. As much as I hate to admit it, I even tried being a so-called "player" once. So, I know all too well how a man's brain functions.

Certain behaviors exhibited by men *and* women can take a toll on a relationship, and it's usually what makes or breaks the dynamics of one. Hopefully you can recall what I said about knowledge and behavior. If you can't, the end of the second chapter will refresh your memory.

I've hardly done everything correctly when it comes to relationships. In fact, I'd describe my voyage through the relationship maze as *adventurous, educational, and riddled with disaster and disappointment, until…* I'll explain this in a bit. I *have* however, done enough to know what does, and doesn't work.

While I'm discussing men, many men will try their *best* to disagree with what I'm saying. At the same time, many women will say I have valid points. Those views are going to invert when I start discussing women. Then, many men will agree, while many women will try *their* best to believe I've gone nuts! That's the price paid for discussing this topic. I'm predicting this, primarily because people tend to agree with statements they're emotionally attached to.

For the record, there will be no previously undiscovered bombshells revealed, here. Many people have heard *what* I'm saying, but they haven't heard it explained *my way!* I can't promise you that my suggestions will result in a wonderful relationship where you live happily ever after, but I'll do my best to put many things into context. Hopefully, it makes it easier to recognize our respective behaviors, and simplifies many of the relationship hurdles we face.

The destiny of a relationship is ultimately determined by your reaction to the circumstances you've been presented. I've mentioned several times that your reaction is the result of a perception driven by emotion, so you should have an idea of what I'm about to say: relationship success or failure is dictated by the thoughts you develop in your head!

Failed relationships have contributed, at least in part to the depression many of us experience as we journey through adulthood. For this book, I'm defining depression as the state created by an abundance of circumstances, on which a person places a tremendous amount of emotional weight, but neither has, or sees a way to control them. Stress is increased, and contributes to the feelings that lead to depression.

I'll contend that there's a way to alleviate much of this stress. You can do yourself a favor by applying what I mentioned in Chapter 4: accept truth for what it is, instead of trying to manipulate it into something you will accept. Try and argue if you want, but here's an undeniable fact: *truth will outlast any lie you can convince yourself to believe!*

I was forced to accept an uncomfortable truth about myself. During my early adult years, I *sucked* at relationships! I didn't want to believe that, but looking back at how each of them unfolded, I discovered the only thing I was good at was taking what was offered to me and being content with it.

What I failed to realize was the amount of effort needed from *me*! As such, I drifted in and out of a number of relationships, always wondering when they ended, *"What happened?!"*

It's simple now, but at the time I didn't realize that each of my failed relationships had a common denominator: *me!* They all went south because of me. Don't confuse this with what occurred that resulted in the relationships ending. Those were the *circumstances*; inanimate entities over which I had no control. I *did* have complete control of my reaction to the circumstances, and that's where the breakdown occurred. I allowed myself to be steamrolled by the circumstances. The actions were the actions, but the inability to communicate clearly rested *solely* with me. It was hard for me to accept and agree with that, but it was a lesson I needed to learn.

When it comes to relationships, usually the biggest complaints I hear from women are, *"There are no good men left,"* *"Men are dogs,"* and *"All the good men are either taken, gay, in jail, or don't know what they want."* From men, it's usually, *"Women are no-good, conniving, emotional, gold digging drama queens."*

Whenever you hear generalized statements like these, you must understand, the majority of the time, they're <u>false</u>! *Of course* there are good men left. Not *all* women are no-good, conniving, emotional, gold-digging drama queens. However, these statements make sense when you're determined to be pissed off, and want other people to co-sign.

As a woman, you haven't met *"all men."* You haven't met enough of all men to be capable of creating an all-encompassing "good" category! So, the *"All the good men are either...*" sentiment is *absolutely* false. If it makes you feel any better, I offer the same argument when I hear men making generalizations about women, because they're just not true.

Generalizations gain momentum because people address them more with emotions than with reason. It's also important to note that a person making a statement like this is trying to solicit emotional responses from other people – another example of the agenda advancement formula.

The moment you buy into these generalizations, your judgment becomes jaded because your emotions aren't being effectively controlled. Your ideals become corrupted and you'll walk around with a chip on your shoulder, because you've chosen to accept a stereotype as fact. This is when you unfairly and *unnecessarily* blame the masses, based on your perception of the actions of a few, and risk shunning good people due to a warped idea you developed in your own head.

Don't get me wrong. I'm not saying stereotypes aren't justified in some cases – though not in *every* case. I've been involved with women who personify every one of those stereotypes. I've been taken advantage of in ways I couldn't have imagined. Those experiences left me hardened towards women, and I adjusted using the only method I knew: exiling myself in my comfort zone. In my mind, no one could hurt me there, and I took my safety to an unnecessary extreme.

I crafted an over-the-top personality, and did everything to maintain my safety, including *lying* to myself. I'd convinced myself that I wasn't looking for a relationship, and made it a point to broadcast it to any woman I even *thought* was showing any interest in me. I didn't want any confusion. I protected myself, but unfortunately, something *else* occurred.

I became someone I didn't recognize. I'd adopted the "player" persona, and feebly attempted to justify it by saying, *"I'm just enjoying being single."* There was one problem... I wasn't any *good* at being a player! I was a smooth talker, but a terrible liar (which is a *wonderful* thing to be, by the way!). My feelings would get in the way, which violates a major rule in the player handbook: *You're not allowed to feel.* I tried living up to the image of a player, but it didn't work for me, at all!

I'm certain my behavior portrayed me as an absolute jerk to many women I met. Many of them were probably not looking for a relationship either, but I didn't care. I wasn't taking a chance on a woman even *thinking* she could get that close to me. Couple this with the outside fuel I received and I thought my attitude was the ideal defense. I thought wrong!

I had several friends who shared the *"Women are no good..."* sentiment. *"Do unto others before they do unto you"* was their motto, and I bought into it hook, line, and sinker! Isn't it amazing how much relationship advice you get from people *not* in a relationship? I said it earlier: *"Misery needs company."*

The issue was my friends' opinions outweighed mine. I put more emphasis on what *they said*, than on what *I thought*. This made it easy to rationalize my behavior, because my friends were verbalizing my thoughts. The confirmation was enough for me to buy into my emotions, and display that awful behavior as my preferred method of protection from heartbreak, and I was okay with that.

My self-imposed exile actually did me a favor. It gave me what I needed – time to re-evaluate my life. I was able to figure out who I was, because at the time, I was struggling to find my "it" factor. I didn't have a massive identity crisis or anything. On the surface, I knew who I was, but didn't know what I wanted. I began asking myself, *"Am I really not looking for a relationship, or am I just telling myself that?"* I've since concluded that it was the latter, and the lessons I learned from asking these two questions are absolutely priceless!

A. Core Principles

Though it seemed harsh at times, the experience of my turbulent relationships has allowed me to discover a unique formula for developing a successful relationship. Personally, I believe people give up on relationships too easily, when it's just as easy to get one to work. Here's what I figured out…

If a relationship is going to succeed, it must be predicated, built, and solidified on *four core principles*. When these principles are the main focus, the odds of success drastically increase. If they're not, the relationship has an uphill climb, and a slim chance of long-term success.

What may surprise some folks about these principles is each of them has *everything* to do with *you*, and *nothing* to do with the other person! That's right… *I said it!* You can contribute to the overall success of a relationship by doing something all by yourself. This goes against every bit of relationship theology you've been led to believe, but by now,

I believe you've read enough to know I'll provide a rational explanation for every crazy-sounding thing I say.

If you are practicing the principles on *your* own, and the other person is practicing them on *their* own, it should be easy to come together and develop a solid relationship. There shouldn't be a lot of tension, because both of you are putting these principles at the forefront. Add your own to the other person's own and you get *two* owns. Figure out a way to make those two "owns" into *"us,"* and it should promote positive relationship growth. *Sounds* easy enough. Can it really be that simple? Not with egos, emotions, and brainpower in the way!

What *are* these magical principles? Valid question, but I have to tell you, there's nothing magical about them, at all! They're common sense ideals I've come up with, to take the guesswork out of developing a healthy relationship. The key is effective management, and this is where balance comes in. You thought I forgot about balance, didn't you? *Not a chance!*

The most important principle is *honesty*. I've emphasized self-honesty from the beginning of the book, but when you add another person to the mix, it's equally as important that you're honest with them. I'm not saying you need to bare your soul immediately after the introductions. However, they should be made aware if you're holding onto emotional baggage from your past, and only *you* know if you're doing it.

If you've had troubled relationships in the past, have trust issues, or are suffering from lingering effects from any type of abuse, the other person has a right to know, and you have an obligation to tell them. They don't need the details, but address it enough so it gives them the opportunity to decide if they wish to continue a relationship with you.

What do you do if you're on the receiving end of this kind of information? If you hear a person constantly referring to, or making comparisons to things from their past, proceed with caution. There may be unresolved internal issues that need to be addressed. If a person reveals this information to you, it's imperative that you're honest as to whether you can handle their baggage or not. If you can't, they need to know.

At the same time, if you tell them you can handle it, you don't get to hold their baggage against them. Your job is to help them *through* it, and you do that with your *actions*. This is why honesty is the most important principle in a relationship.

The next principle is *trust*. Without it, you have nothing to build a relationship on. You must be confident enough to say you're capable of being a significant part of a lasting relationship. You must do your part to ensure things are taken care of on your end, because that's all you control.

You trust yourself, but that's only part, and likely, the easiest part of the trust principle. The more frightening task is opening yourself up, and fully putting your trust in another person. You must be able to say, *"This is my teammate and I trust they'll do right by me, for us."* If you can't emphatically say (and *believe*) this, you may want to pump the brakes, because you're not ready to proceed with a relationship. One of two things is out of whack: you're either involved with the wrong person, or you need to conduct an honest self-assessment.

The third principle is *respect*. In my opinion, this is the craftiest of the four. This is because many people twist its meaning, due to their perception of it. It's been translated many ways by different people, and to different degrees.

"You have to give respect to get respect." This is a sentiment usually expressed by younger generations, though seasoned people express it as well. I'm going to stir the pot a bit by inserting some irony into this mentality. It supports my idea that what gets people most bent out of shape when it comes to respect is created and developed in their own head.

The United States Marine Corps employs an unofficial motto which states, *"Respect isn't given. It's earned."* For the most part I agree, but it contradicts the "give respect to get it" mentality, and can generate an unnecessary impasse in a relationship. You won't give respect to a person until they've earned it from you. At the same time, they won't give you respect because you haven't given it to them first. The irony in all of this is… *respect isn't earned until it's given!*

These are the struggles that occur in many relationships, and usually contribute to the majority of issues within them. One feels they're contributing more to the relationship than the other. This breeds the tit-for-tat perception, and spurs an assignment of a large amount of emotional weight. By now, you know this not only triggers large emotional responses, but also gives neglect a chance to make an appearance.

"I do _____, so you should be doing _____." If you've ever said anything close to this, you'll want to pay close attention to what follows. It's important you understand

how a statement like this can be received by another person. Regardless of what you meant when you said it, most likely, here's what the person heard: *"What I think you should be doing should be a higher priority to you than what you think you should be doing. What I want is more important than what you want!"*

By saying things similar to *"I do... so you should..."* what you've essentially done (at least in the receiver's mind), is discounted their actions in favor of your own, as I did with my team in Chapter 5. Right, wrong, or indifferent, from *their* viewpoint, you've tossed their worth aside, and diminished their significance in the relationship. You're *"keeping score."* *Congratulations...* you've created an unnecessary obstacle that didn't exist, and put it where it didn't need to be!

Each person in a relationship has a role. If these roles aren't clearly defined and adhered to, one will inevitably drift out of *their* role, and into the other. This almost *always* leads to trouble, because people are fiercely defensive of their roles.

I compare relationship dynamics to driving a car. You're not supposed to jump behind the wheel and begin driving. You must first learn some rules so you don't end up killing yourself, or anyone else! The first rule is to respect the car and your surroundings. You may not know where the hazards are, but if you're prepared for them before you begin driving, you can keep an eye out, and possibly avoid them.

Two important rules of driving are: stay in your lane, and signal *before* you change lanes. The latter lets drivers in other lanes know your intentions in advance, and they can prepare for your action. You then check your mirrors and blind spots, and when it's safe, make a smooth transition into the other lane, turn off your signal, and continue driving. This sequence makes things go smoothly, but unfortunately, many people have shown a tendency to suddenly change lanes without signaling, causing others to react erratically in a panic.

In a relationship, you are no more important than the other person, and they are no more important than you. Without a plan to execute quality collaborative teamwork, the relationship is doomed. You must respect the other person's individuality as much as you respect your own.

Each person in a relationship has their respective beliefs, opinions, abilities, aspirations, and activities they enjoy. Are you aware of *theirs*, and support them? Are they aware of *yours*, and support them? If they don't (or *you* don't), a conversation needs to occur, quickly! They're important to the person, and if you *routinely* dismiss, discount, or ridicule them, because they don't mirror *yours*, I can promise, they will become withdrawn, or limit their communication with you.

I said *support*, not *agree with*. It's possible to support without agreement, though agreement helps. As long as the person isn't breaking the law, or hurting anyone by participating in the activity, you can support them, even if you have no interest in the activity, yourself. Why? Your support gives them the green light to strive to be better, and *you'll* benefit from having a motivated person around you. Regular dismissal of, or chiding their interests means instead of enjoying them, they'll be busy *defending* them, which puts them at risk of getting "stuck," or even becoming resentful to you.

The fourth principle is equally as important. Along with honesty, trust, and respect, there must be *self-discipline*. It may sound strange, but starting a relationship isn't the hard part. Deciding to remain in a relationship is where the challenge is presented, and where self-discipline becomes an integral part of the equation. It determines the amount of difficulty you experience in deciding to remain in a relationship.

If relationship trouble begins, you can bet money it's because one or more of these principles has been damaged by someone's actions, causing it to lose its value. However, do you remember when I told you the principles have nothing to do with the other person? They *still* don't! What really happens is the principle gets devalued by *you*, which creates a major roadblock on the journey to a successful relationship. I know that one is tough to take, but hopefully once you read my explanation, you'll understand why I say your mindset can be the cause of most of the damage in a relationship. As the primer for my explanation, try this: the value of each principle can be adjusted by you in an instant, at *any* time, to *any* level!

Self-discipline is probably the easiest principle to repair once it's been damaged, because it only takes a shift in your mindset to correct it. Honesty is a bit more complex. Once honesty has been damaged, it's nearly impossible to completely repair. Sure, the person may forgive you for an indiscretion, but from that point on, in their mind, a tinge of doubt will be attached to everything you say and do. This ties directly to trust. They may never tell you this, so I will, because you need to know: if they're internally questioning what you say or do, they don't trust you with very much.

The principle that causes the most significant damage once it's been devalued is respect. It triggers a chain of events. When the respect level decreases, the tolerance level also plummets. This means the likelihood of anger *increases*. If either (or both) happens, believe me... any, and everything the person does or says will get on your nerves! The simplest actions will infuriate you. There is little, if anything they can do to satisfy your demands, because the core principles will be overridden by emotion, which amplifies your reaction to what they say or do. Anger will blind you to where you aren't listening to *anything* the other person is saying. You will figuratively paralyze yourself by over-assigning emotional weight, and likely choose to kill a spider... with a *shotgun!*

It's important to be cognizant of how you perceive circumstances. Experiences from failed relationships have left many people with lingering trust issues. Judging by the way many relationships have ended, it's easy to see how it can happen. It's also one of the main reasons why I wave the BS flag at something I call a widely-accepted relationship myth: remaining friends following a breakup.

I've heard of couples who've claimed to remain friends after breaking up. I've even seen couples break up and continue to live together. If this works for them, *great*, but personally I find it hard to believe. Breakups aren't easy. They're extremely difficult. Sometimes, they're downright ugly. Think about it: one person wants to leave the relationship while the other person wants to stay. This isn't an easy pill to swallow if you're the one who wants to stay.

The longer you've been in a relationship, the harder it is to come to the conclusion to end it, and regardless of what you try to convince yourself, a relationship *never* ends well. Otherwise... it *wouldn't end!* Each person walks away with a degree of failure, and in nearly every case, one person feels the sting much heavier (and longer) than the other. Let's look at how one of these alleged "easy" breakups unfolds.

One person decides they no longer want to be emotionally attached to the other. Following a discussion, argument, or whatever you'd like to call it, a decision is made to end the relationship. In the midst of that decision, a suggestion to remain friends is made. An agreement is reached and everyone is happy, right? If only it *were* that easy!

Notice how I worded the last paragraph. *A* discussion happened. *A* decision was made. *A* suggestion was made. I did that intentionally, to show that while events did occur, the solutions may have been *assumed*, and not mutually agreed to.

For doubters of my explanation, consider these questions: If you don't want to be emotionally attached to another person, how in the world can you be their friend? Doesn't being friends with someone kind of *require* an emotional attachment? This is why I say people keep trying to make relationships more difficult than they need to be.

In case you wanted to believe otherwise, a relationship doesn't end out of the blue. A lot of thoughts circulate before it gets to that point. A person doesn't wake up one day, and in an instant, say to their significant other, *"I don't want to be with you, anymore,"* pack up and leave. A lot happens before then. An unfortunate end to the relationship could have been averted, if certain things were brought up before it got to the point of no return, preventing a lot of prolonged anguish.

I'll offer this advice to the person who wants to stay in a relationship when the other person wants to leave: If your significant other tells you they no longer want to be with you, nothing you're going to say at that moment will change their mind. When you try to change their mind, you must realize you'll be speaking *emotionally*. This does nothing but promote panic inside you. Furthermore, you'll say, do, and promise things you normally wouldn't. This makes the breakup *more* difficult because you'll be displaying signs of desperation.

The impact is amplified if the person isn't receptive to your offer. I'll be the first to tell you a breakup will hurt for a while. Sometimes, it'll hurt for a *good* while, but the most productive thing you can do for yourself is take the "L" with your dignity intact, and begin the process of healing from it.

People not saying what they really mean can be part of the blame for many of the trust issues. The "soft letdown" leaves a lot of room for ambiguity, mixed messages and misinterpretation. These can cause a person to develop unfounded assumptions (again, in their head), and spur false hope. When the hope doesn't work out the way they planned, they become jaded about relationships due to an emotionally-triggered perception. This is why I believe the "remain friends after a breakup" claim is one of the biggest loads of garbage. Stop buying into this delusion! There is *no* such thing as an easy breakup.

I was in that hardened category, with a lot of trust issues, stemming from both real and imagined circumstances. Failed relationships took me through a lot of disappointment. I know how hard it is to rebound, and wouldn't wish that on anyone. I didn't experience an unrelenting tragedy during a relationship that I couldn't recover from. I've seen people go through much worse than me. I'm now able to recognize, the emotional weight I assigned to those situations is what made them appear larger than they were. Their severity was felt due to my uncontrolled emotions, *not* the circumstances.

Some people will disagree with this, but I believe if you breakup with someone you should close that chapter, period. My position is rather ironic, since I know people who have successfully reconciled with an ex, and are extremely happy. I'm genuinely happy for them. Again, I say if it's working for them, *great!* As with any rule, there are always exceptions, though the percentages are small in comparison.

The major issue I have with reconciling with an ex is one of two things must happen: You must admit *you* were at fault, and take responsibility for the breakup, or you must excuse their behavior during the relationship. In either case, you absolve them from wrongdoing, and ignore the fact that the person irritated you enough, for you to say you no longer wanted to be with them.

Techniques and tactics can always be changed, but a person can't run from their personality if they wanted to. Therefore, the bottom line is when you reconcile with an ex, the only thing that really *changes*… are your expectations!

Letting go of a relationship is easier said than done. There are people who don't know when or how to let go when the relationship is over, but letting go is the only way to begin healing. I'm not saying block out all recollection and forget the person exists. That's impossible to do. I'm saying your healing can't begin *until* you let go. If you can't (or won't), you'll be stuck in a cycle that is extremely difficult to break away from, due to the emotions lent to the situation. This can lead to stalking, an issue I won't even touch. I can't and won't speak for the deranged fool who *refuses* to let go!

I remember seeking my dad's advice following a bad break-up. I was relieved an unfavorable situation ended, but devastated by the circumstances that led to its end. I knew he'd be 100% authentic with his response and he didn't disappoint. What he said is funny as hell now, but when he said it, I didn't want to hear it. Fortunately, he didn't care about telling me what I wanted to hear. He told me what I *needed* to hear: *"If people didn't believe their ex was acting like a jackass, they wouldn't be an ex! There's a reason people are exes, and it ain't because they're nice! You have never heard anybody say, 'You are perfect for me... but I don't want you'."*

Man, did *that* put things in perspective! But *who* was the jackass? Since I didn't have control of what *she* did, I had no alternative but to look at myself. That's when the situation started to shift. I began evaluating my behavior and making adjustments to regain my dignity. I took time to firmly define what I would, and wouldn't tolerate in a relationship. For the most part, these adjustments have made relationships easier.

Think about some of the people who've been married or in a relationship for many years. Do they have a secret formula for success? In a manner of speaking, *yes*. In addition to the principles of honesty, trust, respect, and self-discipline, they've realized that *staying* in a relationship is a decision you have to make *every... single... day!* Do not adjust your eyes, because you did *not* misread it!

Every day, you must decide if you're going to remain in the relationship or not. Once your decision is made, you need the self-discipline to do what's necessary to reinforce the decision. This is where many people stumble. If you ignore, flip-flop, or shy away from your decision, you either have a low self-discipline level (which you may want to work on), or you haven't learned the lesson about lying to yourself.

Don't get the wrong impression and think you have to *agonize* over this, daily. You don't! The more satisfied you are with your significant other, the easier it is to stay. Once you're completely satisfied, the decision is automatic, not agony. Equally, the more *dissatisfied* you are, the easier it is to *leave*.

The four core principles are the foundation for a successful relationship, and as stated earlier, have the one aspect in common: each of them is facilitated through you. So, if both people are making the principles a priority, the relationship shouldn't fail, right? In theory this is correct, but as you'll see in the coming pages, it doesn't always work out that way...

B. The Woman's Behavior

Who's at fault if/when a relationship fails? The man? The woman? Both? It'll depend on who you ask first, because each will play the blame game. He'll blame her. She'll blame him. On the chance one of them admits they're at fault, they usually follow their admittance with some sort of justification: *"Okay it was my fault, but I did what I did because..."* Ladies and gentlemen, I present another example of deflection. Their action was warranted, because of what the *other* person did! See... it's easier to assign blame than to take responsibility.

Men and women need to understand a few things about one another. If you don't know at least some of them beforehand, and have effective pre-emptive actions in place to combat them, it can turn disastrous. Let me explain this.

It's appropriate that I discuss women first, for chivalry's sake. There are certain characteristics many women display that can severely hamper a relationship. I'll be highlighting a number of them, so you get a better understanding of them. I'm not out to shame anyone. Women, I *promise* not to leave men out of the discussion. However, I will be emphasizing the emotional aspects of a relationship, because from a man's perspective, most of the emotional obstacles in relationships are put there by women. Some of them will be hard to accept, or agree with, but try to stay with me.

If you take nothing else away from this chapter, please remember: *men and women communicate differently.* That's not to imply men *or* women are better at relationships. We simply communicate differently. The confusion occurs when one doesn't (or refuses to) understand the methods of the other.

Generally speaking, a woman addresses an issue driven by her emotions. She's great at taking an event, statement, or action, and attaching an emotion to it. This makes a strong impact, and can cause a woman's mind to go from calm to catastrophe in a *millisecond!* The problem is once she's gone "nuclear," she can stay there for an extended period of time. Additionally, if you haven't gone nuclear *with* her, not only is the situation upsetting her, but she's laying into *you* as well!

On the other hand, a man generally addresses issues driven by logic. Most surface issues won't affect a man in the same manner as they would a woman. I'm not... I repeat, *not* saying women are illogical! I'm saying on average, women tend to be more emotional about subjects than men.

In addition to the emotional obstacles, women often communicate in what I refer to as their "code." This means a woman will say something, but *mean* something completely different than what she says. What's interesting about this code is it's usually only recognized and understood by other women! Men are usually left completely in the dark about it.

So, not only is she communicating using a method he doesn't understand, she spends a lot of time searching for complexity in his communication. This is usually a mistake. She's looking for subliminal meanings, trying to speculate on what he's saying. *"Oh... so what you're trying to say is _____."*

While this is going on, she expects him to decipher this women-only code, and adjust his communication to her, accordingly. When he gets the "deer in the headlights" look, she gets upset. Why? It's because of what's in her head! My goodness, how many times have I indicated this now?!

Most men prefer simple methods of communication. We prefer things in our face. If they're not, many men will miss them, because we're usually more literal. For example, we'll say, *"What do you want?"* which vastly differs from *"So what you're trying to say is _____."* Men don't like digging for what we're looking for, especially in a relationship. We prefer things plainly laid out. This is in stark contrast to the complexity a woman may be looking for.

I'm about to reveal something to women, almost every man is aware of. I alluded to it in an earlier chapter, but I think it's important for women to understand this: the *overwhelming* majority of men are *problem solvers*. We want issues resolved, and will do everything we can to achieve that. This applies to chores, and other household tasks. We want these things completed quickly for only *one* reason: *so we don't have to hear your mouth about it!* That's not to be mean, either. We just don't like a bunch of issues lingering.

Ladies here's an important note, and this is as simple as I can put it: if you want to complain about something, vent, or want us to "just listen," you must let us know that, up front! If you *don't*, we will try to resolve whatever issue you bring up. That's how a man's brain is wired.

If you tell us something in a panic, we want it to stop, right then and there! Most men will do their best to keep their woman from reaching a fever pitch, because he knows if she reaches that nuclear level, the entire atmosphere goes awry in an instant! At that point, he's no longer listening to what she's saying. He's looking for a way... *any* way, to calm her down! Why? Because of *this* saying: *"If Mama ain't happy, ain't nobody happy!"* You think someone just pulled that out of thin air?!

These thought patterns are what keep men and women confused about one another. Figuratively speaking, we don't speak the same language. Maybe it's by design, but these communication gaps between the genders are what can put a damper on the dynamics of any relationship.

For example, a woman will ask a "loaded" question that she doesn't really want an answer to. Yet, she'll ask it anyway, and truly expect the man to give her one. This is the code I've been referring to. Watch how one of these loaded question situations can unfold.

"Do these pants make me look fat?" Here's a question many women have asked, and almost every man who's ever been asked the question just *cringed*. It's because both of them know there is no right answer to the question, and the man who's been asked it before knows he's stuck between a rock and a hard place. What can he do? Men, pay attention: I'm going to try and help you make some sense out of this.

A woman asking a question like this already has a pre-determined answer in her head. She's looking for her answer to be validated. To bait him, she might say something like,

"You can be honest. I won't get mad." Now, he's faced with a decision. Does he answer her honestly, or tell her a lie? The truth is, he's in trouble, regardless of his response. How so?

Let's say he thinks the pants indeed make her look fat, and he answers *yes*. For his "honesty," he's rewarded with an infinite amount of grief, for an infinite amount of time. His response will cause her to assign an enormous amount of emotional weight, thus, burning it into her memory *forever!* Rest assured he will *never* forget the time he said she was fat, even though it's *not what he said!* It's what *she heard!* Remember that from Chapter 2? Just so we're clear... he answered a question about a pair of pants, *not* her appearance!

On the other hand, maybe he doesn't want to hurt her feelings, or he truly *doesn't* believe the pants make her look fat, and he answers *no*. If she already has it *in her head* that those pants make her look fat, and *his* answer doesn't match her *anticipated* answer, he gets jumped on and accused of lying!

The pants weren't really the subject of her question. They were simply the tool used at the time to justify the action. Truthfully, he was doomed with either answer, but why would she ask a question like this, anyway? I'll explain that in a moment, but let me point something out, first...

There is no right *answer* to that question, but there is a right *response* which should be as effective. A suitable response would be something like: *"Why would you think I'm that shallow? I'm in a relationship with <u>you</u>, not a pair of pants! I like you the way you are. Now, to your question, I could answer yes or no, but it wouldn't make any difference, because we see things differently. Truthfully, it* *doesn't matter what I see. What matters is what <u>you</u> see!"* Any variation of this should get him off the hot seat. If it doesn't, she's looking for a reason to be upset, and wants *him* to give her that reason, so *she's* not the one who looks crazy!

Another way a woman can sabotage her relationship journey is by believing her initial assessment of a man. I can *imagine* the side-eyes I'm getting, right now! Ladies, before you start cutting me to pieces, read my explanation. For those who think I've lost my mind... I assure you, I haven't!

I need to be clear: I'm not suggesting that any woman ignore her instincts! Most of the time, instincts can keep you out of trouble. The issue is many women pay more attention to the *perceived* instincts than the actual ones. What I mean is they'll follow the instinct that falls most closely in line with their way of thinking. Collectively, women are *notorious* over-thinkers, and this can have an adverse effect on an otherwise pleasant relationship. How does this happen?

Every woman was once a young lady. From an early age she has spent a significant amount of time envisioning her ideal man. Why? It's ingrained in her to do it! Read a fairytale. In those featuring a princess, the princess usually overcomes adversity to find Prince Charming and lives happily ever after.

Need further confirmation of how deep-rooted this vision can be? Ask a woman to describe her ideal man for you. Without blinking an eye, she can tell you his height, weight, career, wardrobe, personality traits, and what kind of car he drives. She can describe him down to the color of his socks! She can even tell you what her wedding dress looks like. It's because she's been envisioning these details since she was little. Okay, I'll admit the socks might be a stretch for most women, but some *will* go that far.

From these constant images, a perception develops in her head, which becomes her expectations. Once these expectations have been formed, every man she meets is measured against them. If he doesn't measure up, he's dismissed, and her search continues. This cycle repeats until she's convinced she's found her Prince Charming.

Unfortunately for the man who's *not* her Prince Charming, this scenario turns out badly more often than not. The only way he knows he's met her expectations, is if a relationship begins. If a relationship doesn't begin, he'll never know what happened because the majority of the selection criteria are in her head. Wait… *what?* Yes, they're in her head!

I've made a statement many times over the years. One day, I may meet someone who proves me wrong, but so far no one has given a legitimate argument that convinces me my statement is inaccurate. Are you ready? Good! *"At some point, every woman has failed a man on a test… he didn't realize he was taking!"* It doesn't have to be romantic, either. It could be her father, uncle, cousin, or whomever – but she's done it. <u>*This*</u> is the reason she asked the question about the pants!

I know the last paragraph may have caught some people (mainly men) off-guard, but this happens, and it happens a lot. It's unfortunate for the man and woman. The man is at a disadvantage, because he has no clue he's being measured against standards that were in place well before he met her.

He's been preparing for a test, but it's likely the *wrong* test! There's no way he could be preparing for *her* test, because he doesn't know what's *on* it. Why? The content is in her head!

On the slim chance a relationship begins despite him failing that "unannounced test," he enters with one strike. He doesn't know he's failed the test, because according to the woman code "rules," she's not going to tell him about it.

This is equally unfortunate for the woman. She knows he isn't going to pass her test, because he's not a mind-reader! Yet she tests him, anyway. When he fails (because of her pre-existing image of Prince Charming) she makes herself believe he doesn't measure up, though he may actually be great for her. He then gets dismissed without a second thought. Why?

She's convinced herself that not only Prince Charming, but *perfect* Prince Charming is waiting for her to cross his path, she'll immediately recognize him, and he'll pass every unannounced test he's unaware he's taking. Sounds crazy, but many women torture themselves like this. It reminds me of a joke. There are multiple versions, but I'll paraphrase one.

A woman visits a store where she can find herself a man. The store has five floors. Patrons are informed at the entrance that each floor contains men with different traits. As the floors increase, the traits are more attractive. There are only two conditions: 1) You can only visit the store once, *ever*, and 2) the elevator only makes stops on the way up. It makes *no* stops on the way down. It goes straight to the bottom floor, and opens to a narrow walkway that leads directly to the exit.

On the first floor, all the men are handsome. Sounds great, but naturally, that's not all she's looking for, so she hops in the elevator. On the second floor, the men are handsome, have great jobs, faithful, and love kids. Again, sounds great, but her perfect prince charming possesses much more than that, so she keeps heading up. On the third floor, they're handsome, have great jobs, faithful, love kids, and work out. On the fourth floor, they are handsome, have great jobs, faithful, love kids, work out, and hopelessly romantic. Almost, but none are quite *"Perfect Prince Charming!"*

The woman can hardly contain herself. She thinks, *"I can't wait to get to the fifth floor! I'll pick my man and be on my way. After all… it's the top floor. The merchandise must be top notch!"* She pushes the button for the fifth floor and heads on up.

When the elevator doors open, her jaw immediately drops to the floor. Instead of the plush, decked-out floor, full of fantastic men to choose from she *expected* to see, she's greeted by an unfinished décor, and a handwritten sign: *"There is nothing on this floor! It was intentionally left unfinished to prove a point — no matter how great the men were on the lower floors, many women will continue looking for a better one! You may now take the elevator to the exit. Good luck in your quest, and thanks for visiting."*

This example, while humorous (I thought it was hilarious), illustrates my point about a woman's image of her ideal man. Many women are fixated on their standards because they've been embedded. A woman can quickly sour on a man when she doesn't think he meets her standards. Never mind that he doesn't know what those standards are!

Another action taken by many women that contributes to relationship chaos and makes it more difficult than it needs to be is presumptive communication. This normally happens when the relationship has been going a while, but can happen at the start if the woman is leery, based on bad experiences.

What the heck is presumptive communication? It has a few meanings, but I'll discuss one. A woman hears a man say something, but processes it in her head to mean something completely different, almost expecting him to be deceitful. Men's collective behavior in failed relationships have spoiled it for those who do it right. Many women have been conditioned to believe they must be detectives when dealing with men. As such, it may take a lot to earn a woman's trust, and even still, you may never fully receive it. Blame it on her past experiences, but more specifically, on the amount of emotional weight she assigns to a person gaining her trust.

To put this into context, consider this: During a conversation the woman asks a question. You already know she's anticipating an answer, thanks to those unannounced tests she likes administering. If his answer doesn't match hers, she interrogates him to level five, when the answer she needed was located on level *two!*

This behavior normally occurs when a woman won't turn her brain off. Notice I said *won't*, and not *can't*. Anyone is capable of whatever they set their mind to, but watch how this common practice by many women often turns out.

If a woman's brain is on all the time, it's constantly working, making it susceptible to fatigue, due to being overworked. This means it is prone to creating hypothetical scenarios from ordinary situations, and if she assigns a large amount of emotional weight to the hypothetical scenario, it becomes real in her head. This is when invented obstacles start popping up. Certainly *resembles* self-sabotage, doesn't it?

Ladies, my point is if you *want* to find something wrong, you'll *find* something wrong! It's that simple. Digging *until* you find something wrong hardly promotes a healthy relationship. If you constantly do this, the man will feel like he's under unwarranted scrutiny. This doesn't bode well in promoting trust, an essential principle to a relationship's foundation.

Men are easier to understand if what we say or do is taken as it's presented. Contrary to popular belief, most men are *not* that complicated. You don't have to be a detective to figure out most men. If you're under the impression that this type of behavior is necessary, perhaps you haven't found Prince Charming, yet. Even if you've been deceived by men in the past, you shouldn't automatically assume every man following the last man will, or even *wants* to repeat the cycle!

Everyone has experienced unfavorable circumstances while searching for the right relationship. It's how we learn what is and isn't attractive to us. Unfortunately, some of those circumstances have a long-lasting impact; we remember them forever. The scars left can run deep, but here's an interesting point: they only run as deep as emotions allow.

I'm offering this advice to women, though many men might find it helpful, as well. Previously failed relationships have long-term emotional effects on us when it comes to starting new ones. Something I alluded to earlier may help you: *"Don't hold your future hostage by creating circumstances with your present actions or decisions, based on bad past experiences."* This can be applied to *any* life situation – not just to relationships!

A woman's image of her perfect Prince Charming may be what's causing the turmoil she's experiencing. After all, she's had him in her mind for years! Is a woman wrong for having standards? No. Should she disregard them and go for the first man who's nice to her? *Absolutely not!* In fact, I'd question her sanity if she did! On the other hand, it may *be* those standards that keep derailing her in relationships.

C. The Man Can Jack Up a Relationship, Too!

Everything that goes wrong in a relationship isn't the woman's fault. Many men have wrecked relationships just as badly. Men don't usually go to as much of an extreme in a relationship as women do with our behavior, but we have our quirks. Generally, men are less dramatic. Don't confuse less dramatic with less impactful. Some of the tactics used by men are as damaging, if not *more* than those used by women.

Here's where I'm going to try to "rescue" women from the figurative ridicule many men have undoubtedly given them as they've read this chapter. It's time I highlighted some of the actions and behavior displayed by men. What's interesting is even though I'm discussing men, a lot of this information can be applied to women, and it would be completely accurate.

I have an answer to a question that's been burning in many women's minds for a while: *"Does a man have something in his DNA that prevents him from building a solid relationship?"* Figuratively speaking, yes, but hold on a second. It isn't hard-wired like his personality, where he can't change it, but similar to a woman, a man's issues have everything to do with *him*, and nothing to do with the other person.

But *unlike* women, you'll be hard-pressed to find a man who tells you he's been envisioning his "Enchanted Princess" since he was young. Most young men can barely think passed that evening's *dinner*, let alone years into the future! We don't usually think that far ahead. If we do, it doesn't involve imagining the type of relationship we want. Our downfall doesn't come from some fantasy woman we've dreamt about since we were six. It comes from an inherent indecisiveness, which I'll certainly explain. Gentlemen: brace yourself for the next few paragraphs. It's going to be a rough ride!

In a good number of cases, a man's issue is, he thinks if he's *in* a relationship, he'll miss out on the "next best thing." This is usually the reason behind the player persona, where he's juggling multiple women, or the constant roaming eye. He may even try to rationalize the behavior with some ridiculous-sounding justification like: *"Monogamy isn't natural; blah, blah, blah…"* Women, don't buy this crap – he's full of it!

This is the type of behavior that usually fuels the highly-anticipated, yet largely unproven perceived deceitfulness women seem to want to clue in on with men. *He* thinks he's missing something, but *she's* busy administering unannounced

156

tests. This is likely why the genuinely nice guy is mistaken for the "dog," and is subsequently taken advantage of by the "no good, conniving, emotional, gold digging drama queen." See how the cycle repeats? It's a miracle we *sustain* relationships!

I believe it can be done, and it's as simple as shifting your mindset. This is where many people (particularly men) become more confused. You think deciphering the woman code is difficult? Try convincing someone to alter their thinking, when they believe their current method is working!

Building a successful relationship begins with properly and *emphatically* defining the traits you find attractive. If you can do this, and find a person who possesses them, you aren't missing anything another person has to offer! You're not missing out on the *next* best thing, because you already have the best thing for you! How? You've determined the traits that make you happy and found the person who *has* them! If that's the case, what are you *missing?* Your selection criteria have been met. Couple this with the foundation of those four core principles, and the long-lasting relationship mystery should be solved. Then, monogamy is *completely* natural.

A woman's standards for her Prince Charming aren't necessarily a bad thing. She must have standards in order to know what she wants. The situation becomes jaded when those standards aren't firmly defined. If this happens, *options* can be mistaken for *requirements*, and they shouldn't be.

Let's say you're a woman who says she's looking for *"tall, dark, and handsome."* If Mr. Tall, Dark, and Handsome walks into your life, you shouldn't dismiss him because he doesn't drive the right kind of car. The car he drives is an *option*. If you dismiss him because of his car, you've made an option a requirement, which is unfair, because you received what you initially asked for. If you were going to measure him by his car, then *"tall, dark, and handsome"* should have been *"tall, dark, handsome... and drives the right kind of car."*

This causes a string of events which usually doesn't end well. Mr. Tall, Dark, and Handsome becomes bitter because he's unaware he "failed" because of the car he drives. He's left to his own devices to make assumptions about what went wrong, which can cause him to change some good qualities into bad ones. He transfers that negative energy to the next woman, who actually *wants "tall, dark, and handsome."* What she gets instead is, *"tall, dark, handsome... and bitter"* because of what's in his head. I've truly lost track of how many times I've pointed this out. See what these undefined standards can do? And here *you* were... only thinking about *yourself!*

Don't worry – men have sabotaged themselves in the same manner! A man wants the woman he's involved with to look good and have a nice figure. That sounds shallow, but since most men haven't spent years dreaming of an ideal woman, physical appearance is what initially attracts him. He finds out about her intelligence, personality, etc., once she starts talking. Let's look at how a man can jack things up...

Ms. *"Looks Good with a Nice Figure"* comes along, and stares a man in his face. He'll check her out from her head to her toes (yes, he looks *that* far). If all of this is to his liking, and she appears to be intelligent, he'll be open to pursuing a relationship (if *she's* willing) but for a while, he'll be trying to validate his decision by searching for a reason to disqualify her. While this battle is occurring, he's keeping an eye out for the *next* Ms. Looks Good with a Nice Figure.

If he settles on a reason, and disqualifies her without revealing the reason to her, she'll follow the pattern of Mr. Tall, Dark, and Handsome, converting good traits into bad ones based on assumption, becoming bitter, and carrying that attitude to the next man. The difference is she thinks she knows what went wrong. How? In *her* mind, he failed "the test," but of course, he didn't know he was taking one.

If he can't find reasonable justification to dismiss her, he moves forward with the relationship, but keeps that ace in his pocket in case he feels he needs to play it, and think he's being slick by doing so. Why does he do this? He isn't being honest with himself about what he wants. Similar to the woman in the store, he's convinced there's something better if he keeps looking, and he's going to stumble upon it, "*soon.*"

Unfortunately, *soon* can turn into weeks, months, and sometimes even *years*! All because he either won't, or hasn't taken time to firmly define the traits he likes, or what he's looking for. If he had, he may have prevented a lot of drama.

What can you do to ensure you're giving a relationship every chance to survive? A great start is recognizing that a relationship will *rarely* be perfect. The person will get on your nerves, and you, on theirs. That's the nature of the beast. If you know this beforehand, you're less likely to fly off the handle about things that don't matter in the grand scheme. Then again, you may be the person who likes to complain.

You may need to do some work on yourself. You shouldn't begin a relationship without first figuring out what you want from another person. If you don't, you'll risk doing one of the most destructive things a person can do to a relationship – *changing the rules in the middle of the game!*

This will have you second-guessing your decision to begin a relationship. You'll start nit-picking at the person over trivial things, like the way they chew their food, reaching for some asinine justification for being upset. Of course, this is again, caused by the emotional weight you assign.

Changing the rules in the middle of the game gets people into trouble a couple of ways. First, it gets them stuck in relationships seemingly going nowhere. The lines of tolerance keep changing positions, so there's no concrete evidence telling them if, or when they should leave. Thanks to the comfort zone and the figurative fear of winning, they stay in a relationship when everything suggests they shouldn't.

Perhaps you know, or have seen this person: they're involved with someone who treats them like garbage. It's apparent to you they can do much better, yet they remain in that bizarre situation, ignoring every clue that suggests they shouldn't be there. They've never been introduced to the person's family, and barely know any of their friends. If and when they're introduced, they aren't "girlfriend," "boyfriend," "man," or "lady." They are "friend," "girl," "guy," or "dude." Despite these warning signs, the person stays put.

This description makes a person sound rather pathetic or desperate, but there are people who exhibit this behavior. Why would a person subject themselves to treatment like this? The answer is they may not know they're doing it. If they do know, there are usually two interesting reasons why.

Number one — out of fear of failure, being alone, facing rejection, that no one else will be interested in them, or any number of reasons, they'll force themselves to be content with the no-good person, no matter how badly they're being treated, so other people can see they have someone. I said content is often mistaken for success, right? They're in familiar terrain — their comfort zone. Secondly, they haven't taken time to firmly establish their selection criteria. As such, they have no idea what they want, or what will satisfy them.

Since they have no idea what they want, they go along with what they receive, hoping *that* miraculously turns into what they want. If it doesn't, they become broken and bitter, bearing those deep emotional scars. Anyone coming along after that will likely end up paying for a scar they had no part in creating. Is that *fair?* Not a bit, but it happens.

If you want to minimize the issues, you must get passed the emotional scars, because they are causing the majority of them. It's possible (because of the scars you've suffered) to emotionally brow-beat a person to the point where they no longer care. This is a mistake, because at *that* point, every action or decision will be driven by emotion, not logic.

In a relationship, you must take a person at their word, until they give you a sufficient reason not to. The current person isn't the last person, and shouldn't be viewed as such, unless they exhibit the last person's behavior. Notice I said a *sufficient* reason. That means a *concrete* reason – not some obscure reason you've concocted in your head!

Imagine the following scenario, which is a fairly common occurrence in many relationships: a woman is with her man, and it's obvious they're a couple. In passing, another woman greets them both, though independently. In the man's mind, this isn't a big issue, but the woman has other ideas. She doesn't feel the woman spoke to her as pleasantly as she did to him. Remember, their code is only recognized by other women. So, what's likely to happen next?

The man will get hassled because his woman *felt* the other woman disrespected her, and he didn't do anything to stop it. The problem is he didn't pay enough attention to the other woman to see anything to stop. He responded to being spoken to by another person. In essence, the woman got bent out of shape because of *her perception*... not *his actions!*

I wouldn't necessarily throw down the insecurity or jealousy card, though the argument could certainly apply. Sometimes we assign so much emotional weight because of past experience, that we'll levy an unfair level of leeriness on the current person as a method of protection. We'll judge them as guilty of an imaginary "crime" based on assumption, because we don't want a repeat of a hurtful past.

This unwarranted protective measure is another way changing the rules of the middle of the game gets people into trouble. I'll reiterate something from chapter 5, if you're regularly reacting to situations at level 10, when the situation only warrants a level 2 reaction, you're using extreme action. As such, a person will eventually scale back the information communicated to you. This sets off a chain of events, because you'll take offense to their action, and unwisely throw wrenches into an otherwise pleasant relationship in response. You'll be protecting yourself, but from *what?*

D. Making Sense of the Chaos

I've heard many people say the reason their past failed relationships went south was because the other person *"changed."* Each time I hear that, I wonder, *"Did the person really change?"* If you recall what I said about a person's personality a little while ago, you already know where this is headed.

Normally, a person can't sidestep their personality without being fraudulent. What changes, are the tactics they use. So, when you say a person changed, what you're really suggesting is something *hard-wired* in the person irritated you enough for you to say they changed. I hate to break it to you, but *they* didn't change – your *expectations* did!

Try to argue if you want, but when you met the person, their personality was on full display (albeit, its *best* display) and you had no problem. Now that you're in a relationship, you want them to change something you initially found *attractive*. You liked the person they were, when you met. However, you no longer like *that* person, and want them to be somebody *else?!* How crazy is that? What if you don't like the "somebody else" your "wants" forced them to become? *Then* what?

163

Their personality is who they are, and have always been. Therefore, it is a *constant*. Your perception is developed in your head. It stems from the emotional weight you assign, and can change with your mood. Therefore, it is a *variable*. I'm reminded of the chemistry experiment where vinegar is added to baking soda. Separately, the elements are harmless, but combining them causes an interesting reaction. Based on this theory, which element is likely to cause the reaction when it's combined with the other – the constant, or the variable?

I've deliberately made repeated mentions of emotional weight because its impact can cause some strange behavior. For example, you can unnecessarily overanalyze things and create issues where there aren't any, to recover from disaster that hasn't happened. Or, you can confuse politeness with flirting, and constantly wonder if, or when the other person will cheat. Or, you can feel like you have to "do everything," then *do* "everything," then *complain* about "doing everything!"

All these things are developed in your head, and cause you to assign emotional weight based on a flawed perception. You'll be reacting to scenarios that don't exist, which like hating imaginary things, will make you look and sound *crazy!*

Again, I'm not saying you shouldn't protect yourself, but in a relationship, you shouldn't feel like the other person is "out to get you." There may be people who are, but your significant other shouldn't be among the suspects. They may be many things, but *"enemy"* <u>CANNOT</u> be one of them! This is how emotional weight can damage a relationship, and I'll remind you, the amount assigned is controlled solely by *you*.

Each person in a relationship is responsible for their own behavior. Until you have *your* behavior controlled, find the person who has done the same, and you *both* understand this is essential to relationship success, sentiments like, *"There are no good men,"* and *"Women are no-good, emotional, conniving, gold digging drama queens"* will continue being spewed.

Neither is true of course, and can cause people to behave like lunatics when it's unnecessary. Your significant other should feel like they're in a partnership, but behaviors like these don't always make it appear that way. Don't believe me? Watch this! Oh… you may want to grab that helmet.

"I do everything around here!" *"You don't do anything around here!"* If you've ever shared a household with another person before, comments like these have been made at some point. These, and others that begin with expressions like, *"I never…"* *"You always…"* *"I always…"* or *"You never…"* can create emotional landslides, because of their emphatic implications.

Never and *always* are powerful (and <u>definitive</u>) words. In their intended context they sound terrible, and justifiably so. The issue is like most generalized statements, they're rarely (if ever) *true!* Their impact is determined by the person's perception of the circumstances, and the amount of emotional weight they've assigned prior to the statement.

If you've made similar statements, it's important you realize the underlying implications. If your helmet is nearby, put it on, because what you're about to read, you probably *"ain't gonna like!"* What you're doing is internalizing the circumstances. It's not that the person isn't doing *anything*. They're just not doing what you *want* them to do!

When you internalize things, what you do is *minimize,* or dismiss what the person is doing, or has done, and *emphasize* what *you* do, as well as (as *you* see it) what they *didn't* do. At this point, the issue is no longer about *them*. It's about *you, your* satisfaction, convenience, or some benefit to *you!* When you make an issue personal, you take a personal stake in it, and react accordingly. Usually, this reaction takes a defensive or aggressive tone, which in turn is perceived as *offensive*.

Instinctively, the other person becomes defensive, to counteract, or neutralize *your* action. Now, the two of you are at an unnecessary standoff, all because the respect principle has been devalued (by *you*), based on *your* decision to evaluate *their* performance by *your* standards. I said you didn't arrive at your current situation by chance, right? Your extreme *approach* dictated the course of the situation, and triggered an extreme *reaction*. I'll reiterate: reactions are *secondary* impulses. They don't just happen. They are *triggered.*

Did you notice I omitted communication, commitment (or lack thereof), finances, infidelity, and other people meddling as reasons relationships sour? Many people insist that these can doom a relationship, and I won't dispute their sentiments. I deliberately left them out, because on their own merits, they don't mean much. Their impact is subjective, and circles back to emotional weight. For example, finances may be important, but emotional weight determines *how* important it is. Communication *is* important, but the value you assign to the core principles dictates *how* you communicate.

Taking some of the following actions will help unravel the relationship mystery. First, you must trust the other person without reservations. This can be terrifying if you've been hurt before, but when a person begins a relationship with you, they're in it until *you* give them a reason not to be. I can promise you, they're *not* wasting their day thinking of ways to antagonize you, in order to make you leave! *Normal* people don't begin a relationship trying to expedite its ending.

That's not to say there aren't justifiable reasons to end a relationship. The key is recognizing which of the reasons are legitimate, and which are being fabricated. Have you seen a relationship end, but have no idea why it ended? It may have been something running through the other person's mind, but it may have been something running through *your* mind!

Yes... it might be your own brain creating the chaos! A crucial element in relationship success is you. If you've had multiple failed relationships while trying to find the right one, at some point, you'll need to ask two questions I alluded to in Chapter 5, *"Is my luck really that bad, and there's something wrong with everybody I date? Or could there be something wrong with me?"*

Realistically, what are the chances of something being wrong with *every* person you date? This is another illustration of possibility vs. probability. There's a *possibility* of something being wrong with every person you date, but the more *probable* argument is there may be something wrong with *you!*

Are you holding onto emotional baggage you didn't realize you were holding? Maybe you realize you're holding it, but are intentionally concealing it, in hopes of not being hurt again. It seems logical, but holding the current person responsible for what previous people did, is making them pay for a debt someone else created – forcing them to pay for *your perception!* Sounds terrible when it's put that way, doesn't it?

By agreeing to begin a relationship you've implied that by your observations, the person meets the majority of your selection criteria. If the selection criteria constantly changes, no one will ever satisfy it, and that's how bitterness is brewed and perpetuated. Had I not learned this, I'd still be stuck in a cycle of failed relationships. Luckily, I uncovered the issue.

My entire approach to relationships was off. I was looking for "Ms. Perfect." As such, none of my relationships lasted because no one measured up to the selection criteria. Why not? It kept changing! I modified it based on my interest level in a woman. If she was *"fine,"* I'd overlook many things that normally would be deal-breakers. What I was actually doing was trying to make myself fit into what I thought was *her* selection criteria. I was prepared for *my* test... not *hers!*

Blinded by physical attraction and emotion, I adjusted my behavior based on my perception of the woman I was interested in. Subconsciously, I made *myself* the obstacle to overcome. I know I'm not the only one who's ever done this.

Other factors to consider are the people around you. They may see things you are oblivious to. When you're into another person and trying to develop a relationship, you may ignore, or "not see" things that are *glaring* to other people. You're too busy trying to see if the person fits your criteria.

For some people this may sting, but the truth is more valuable than months, or even years of horrible treatment in a relationship. If the majority of people in your circle express a concern about the person you're involved with, you have to look at things logically. There's something to be said when family and friends are strongly opposed to the person. Wait... they don't "know" them like *you* do. That *has* to be it, right?! See how we can fool ourselves with what's in our head?

Do you really believe it's a coincidence that people who haven't spoken to (or know) each other would come to the same conclusion? If numerous people in your circle are adamant that there may be something wrong with the person, there may be something wrong with them. Multiple people usually don't come to a mutual conclusion about the same thing, without there being at least an inkling of truth to it.

I'm all for being with whomever makes you happy, but logically speaking, what is the probability of a *group* of people all being wrong about the same thing? As long as you know they're not a bunch of haters, at least consider what they say. The person may indeed be "the one," but if there is *that* much initial opposition from people you trust, have a conversation to clear up any concerns. If that many people are mistaken, it should be easy to address and resolve.

Unfortunately, many people choose not to have this conversation. They don't want to face the possibility that their judgment may be errant. As a result, they stay in a relationship headed nowhere, much longer than they should.

It took a few years of beating my head against the wall before I started using this experience to my advantage. Two important steps I took were to *stop* looking for "Ms. Perfect," and *start* looking for "Ms. Perfect *for me.*" Once I did, my wife fell right in my lap! When we became a couple, I noticed family members and friends weren't saying *"something's not right"* or they *"just don't like her."* I defined my criteria, and found a woman who fit it, without me trying to *make* her fit.

I can say without hesitation, I'm not missing anything any other woman has! I don't have the slightest romantic interest in another woman, because my wife satisfies <u>all</u> my selection criteria. Another woman may not satisfy *any* of it, and I'm not willing to test the theory! No other woman is more perfect for me. I've established the qualities I like, and determined my wife has them. That's it, and that's all!

I've been 100% *all in* with my wife since the day we became a couple. It's because of *this*, a woman trying to subtly flirt with me in hopes of me stepping out, has *two* problems to deal with: Number 1, I'm a man. Men don't see subtle... *at all!* Number 2, if I recognize a woman is being flirtatious, I have no problem telling her to go straight to *hell!* I'm not trying to impress her, and couldn't care less if she gets mad!

Of course, my wife will see the woman's actions much differently, because of that code of theirs. However, I don't pay any attention to another woman's actions, because quite frankly, *I don't need to!* I'm with the woman I want, and I firmly believe in, *"A bird in hand is worth two in the bush."*

My wife isn't perfect, nor am I. We have ups and downs like everyone else. There are times when she gets on the *last nerve I have*, and I'm certain I get on hers. We both admit we're sometimes difficult to deal with. However, since I believe she satisfies my selection criteria, and I predicate my role in our relationship on those four core principles, barring infidelity, I *refuse* to entertain the idea of divorce, again! The decision to stay is *truly* as easy as opening my eyes every day. I believe my wife is perfect *for me*, and that's *enough* for me!

Hopefully, I've been able to shed some light on a few major relationship obstacles. If you've been in what feels like an endless series of disastrous relationships, the issues may not have been caused by another person, but by the devalued core principles, or the selection criteria you failed to define. So how do you shift the odds to favor a healthy relationship?

For starters, understand you only control what you *can* control – *you!* You can't stop a person from being a jerk in a relationship. If the person is going to cheat, they'll cheat, regardless. Secondly, you don't *make* someone cheat. They make a *choice* to do it! Besides, people cheat for only one reason: in their mind, something is missing from their current relationship, and believe they can find it with someone else; has little to do with what the current person did, or didn't do.

Next, if the person is going to be abusive, whether it's physically, emotionally, or otherwise, they'll be abusive, regardless. This is a character flaw they need to work on, but not at *your* expense! Remember this, and it's not a typo: *"Hurt people hurt people!"* You cannot, and should never blame yourself for another person's actions or behavior. Your responsibility is to ensure *you* are squared away. An excellent start is by learning to laugh again. Put this element back in your arsenal if you've noticed it hasn't been there in a while. For me, there's no better sound than my wife's laughter, and better feeling, knowing I am the *cause* of it!

If your relationship has failed, or is troubled, remember, it began *pleasantly*. There were things you enjoyed. When these are forgotten or neglected, is when the rules get changed mid-game. Again I ask, *"Did the person really change,"* or could the expectations *you created* made them <u>appear</u> to change, or, could *your* actions have caused them to change their *tactics?* You must ensure your response isn't really a *flawed perception.*

Learn to stop taking things so seriously! Crafting conspiracy theories to justify the invention of obstacles is a coping mechanism. It may be the person's nature to smile, or be nice to people. It doesn't mean they're flirting. Most times, this is called being *polite!* Here's something else to consider: the actions you're belly-aching about… attracted *you!* They were okay back then, but now they're *not? C'mon!*

Stop creating issues where they don't exist, because of assigning a lot of emotional weight to, or needing to control a situation. This applies to constantly looking for things to be pissed off about, keeping score, and reacting to everything at once, too. You will *always* put more value on what *you've* done. Think about the effects of stacking. You are *going* to react differently to five things going wrong, as opposed to one.

Will you have arguments or disagreements? *Absolutely!* That's the nature of the beast. It's okay to have them. In fact, you should expect them, but it's also important to know how to disagree, discuss, argue, fight, or whatever you call it, *fairly.* This means you should be listening more than you speak, which can be difficult during an argument (particularly for many women), because people (mainly men) will shut down quicker than a *hiccup* if they feel they aren't being listened to.

I was taught, *"You were born with two ears and one mouth for a reason. You should listen twice as much as you speak!"* What you hear may alleviate the problem, but doesn't have a chance, if you're constantly talking yourself into a frenzy! You *can't*, no matter how hard you try... talk and listen at the same time! *"Oh... you want to talk. You don't want to listen! I'll shut up and wait for you to finish,"* is what most men are thinking when their woman reaches that nuclear level. Problems persist when (or if) she never finishes, or comes *down* from nuclear!

You have to stop dragging up things (past *or* present), if the *only* thing they do is make you mad. When you're regularly getting mad at events that occurred sometimes even *years* ago, you are intentionally reliving them, so they may as well have occurred five *minutes* ago!

What other purpose does constantly bringing them up serve? Maybe you enjoy being eternally mad!? It does you no *good*, but because you're in your comfort zone, you feel power and significance, but here's what you *don't* see: while you're still mad about what *happened*, you're *not* paying attention to what's *happening*, and *stalling your own progress!* If you're getting

173

mad about things, but not doing much, if anything to change or correct them, you don't want a *fix*... you want to be *mad!*

Is your instinctive strategy, *"defend, counter-punch, and attack"* even in "normal" situations? No matter what's been done, what *hasn't* been done sticks out, and *that's* what you focus on? It's safe to conclude what I wrote earlier – the issue isn't the person, *or* the task. It's the emotional weight you assign. As much as you'd like it to be something else, your cookie-cutter expectations and lack of satisfaction are the stumbling blocks. I'll again point out, *both* these things are in your head! Remember, your approach dictates the situation's direction. *Reactions* are responses to your approach.

It's no secret how and why these situations come about. You want *what* you want, *when* you want it, and want to talk about what you want, when *you* want to talk about it! When you feel you can't, you respond. The issue (as unpleasant as it may sound) is at that moment, your focus is on *you*, with little regard for the other person. In case you forgot: Everyone doesn't *have* to want what you want, when you want it, or talk about what you want, when *you* want to talk about it!

Anytime you want to try and dispute this theory, I challenge you to do something you were likely taught as a child. Employ emphatic self-honesty, and put yourself in the other person's shoes. Run your response again, and see if you'd appreciate what you said, if someone said it to *you*. If you would, great! If you *wouldn't*, the other person probably received it the same way. Words can cut deep, and once they've been said, you don't control how they're perceived.

Next, you have to stop getting mad at people for doing things *you* do! You don't get to be mad when somebody pulls a "you" on *you!* This is why I've depicted self-honesty as such an imperative trait. Coming to terms with your own behavior and beliefs will provide you with insight into whether you're reacting to an issue, or reacting to your *perception* of the issue.

Your significant other (or *any* other) cannot, and should *never* be forced to compete with what you create in your head. They lose that battle, *every* time! A person can only be held responsible for what they say or do – *not* for how you *perceive* it! Thinking otherwise is unfair to them... *and* you!

If issues are lingering from your past, let the other person know about them before they surface during a heated, emotional discussion. Listening is your friend. The person's response may be what you need to be able to set the burden down and walk away – permanently, and without worry!

Stop trying to "recover" from disaster that hasn't *happened*. There's no way to predict disaster. You can only manage your response to it. Keeping your brain on all the time does you no good, so give it a break! Don't, and you'll continue over-analyzing situations – "finding" and reacting to things that may not be there. If you can't, or refuse to see how perception can affect a situation, re-read Chapter 5.

Lastly, if a relationship is going to end, it's going to end. There's nothing you can do about it. As long as you've done everything you can on your end, the best thing to do is insist that the other person give you their reason for ending it. Don't *invent* a reason for them! You give them an easy out if you do that. If they give you *their* reason, you won't drive yourself crazy like I did, wondering if you caused the collapse.

Still feel trapped in a cycle of failed relationships? I'll again stress the importance of balance. Check to see if you're properly employing the core principles as the nucleus of the relationship. Are you unjustifiably devaluing any of them?

The person you share a relationship with needs to feel needed. Your words and actions *should* reassure them of this. It's *unreasonable* to expect smiles and cheers from *them*, if what they're regularly hearing from *you* is how much of a burden, inconvenience, or obstruction they are to you, or other belittling language and you're doing *nothing* to shift that, other than complaining. You're practically *pushing* them to the "don't care" point. Soon, outside distractions will walk into your relationship, and *you'll* be the one holding the door open!

I equate the four core principles to the structure of a house. It's impossible to build a solid house unless everything is firmly in its respective place. *Honesty* is the foundation. It must support the weight of the entire structure. The windows represent *trust*. They are easily broken, and a pain in the butt to repair. *Respect* is the framework. If it's not sturdy enough to support the roof (*Self-discipline*), everything comes crashing down, and you're left with a heap of mangled scrap material.

Here's something else to chew on: *"If you don't like the fish you're catching, change the bait you use!"* Catfish tastes great when it's seasoned and cooked properly, but one of the most effective baits to *catch* one... smells like a *dirty diaper pail!*

176

8. Peer Pressure

"Man, stop being a punk!" "I bet you won't..." "I wouldn't take that if I were you!" "Go ahead... I dare you!" "Oh, I knew you wouldn't." Do any of these sound familiar? Most people have heard one of these, or something similar at least once in their life. If you're lucky, you've only heard them once.

I wasn't that lucky. I've heard all of these, and then some. I've caved into them many times, and had to deal with the consequences for doing so. It wasn't to the point of being dangerous, but in hindsight, some of the situations I found myself in could have been handled more responsibly.

Comparing my adolescence and early adult years to my life and mindset now, I didn't always have the same reaction to what I now know as peer pressure. On many occasions, I fell victim to it and ended up doing things I had no business doing. Most people can admit they've behaved similarly at various points, but I did it *a lot*. The difference between who I was and who I am is I now have the ability and confidence to tell a person to take a long walk off a short pier.

Don't get things twisted. I had limits to what I'd do. I wouldn't break the law, or jeopardize my safety for anybody's enjoyment, but almost anything short of that, I'd probably give it a shot. I can laugh about it now, because I know I was being silly, as most young adults are when they think they're invincible. However, the circumstances I was wrestling with mentally at the time were *hardly* a laughing matter.

I did a lot of maturing in the Air Force, but it wasn't a rapid process. There were quite a few instances where peer pressure manifested itself in the form of challenges. Most were harmless fun, but others were real tests of my tenacity.

I fell under the spell of peer pressure frequently as a young adult, and now I can identify the reason for my doing so. I was fresh out of an unsuccessful marriage that happened way too early, and struggling to find my niche. Internally, I was a train wreck, and my self-esteem was in the gutter. However, my work performance remained stellar. My co-workers never knew much about my inner struggles, and I did everything I could to keep it that way, because depression wasn't going to pay any of my bills.

I made what I believed were some good friends during this period, but unfortunately, I was more concerned with those friends' acceptance than with self-honesty. I wanted to belong, because inside I felt lost. As such, it didn't take much for me to fold under peer pressure. During my naïve stage, the only thing a person needed was the "trigger word."

You may have a different word or phrase, but for me, the word was *punk*. Whenever I heard it, a bell went off in my head. I became determined to prove I wasn't anybody's punk. It seems asinine now, but I assigned a massive amount of emotional weight to that word. It was because of this and the sheer *stupidity* I had in me at the time, I engaged in some of the absolute *dumbest* behavior known to man! Whether it was drinking too much too fast, or some other senseless stunt, once the trigger word was dealt, it was game-on.

I'm certain my friends enjoyed some tremendous laughs at my expense. Most likely, because they couldn't believe I was actually doing what they dared me to do! I can't fault them. If I saw someone *willing* to entertain me by engaging in asinine behavior, I would have done the same thing.

In the midst of all that reckless (and might I add *stupid*) behavior, I began receiving glimpses of clarity, and questions start forming in my head. Not about *what* was I doing, because *that* I knew. I start wondering why I was the one being challenged. Why weren't these so-called friends doing the asinine things they were asking me to do? They knew I'd accept the challenge, and voluntarily become their source of mindless entertainment.

Why is peer pressure so difficult for some people to deal with? What occurs in the mind of a person who constantly caves into it? These are legitimate questions, and now that I've gotten wiser, the reasons people succumb to peer pressure amaze me. Here's my take on what happens when a person allows peer pressure to get the best of them. It may provide a different perspective on the behavior.

When you cave into peer pressure, what happens is you initially make a decision you're comfortable with, but opt instead to go with another person's suggestion. You second-guess your own judgment in favor of somebody else's, and hope their judgment is correct. To put it another way (and this may sting a little), what you're doing is communicating a message to the other person that for a brief moment, *they* have more control over your life than *you* do!

Coming to this realization hit me like a stomach punch, but it's exactly what happened each time I accepted one of those ridiculous challenges. When you allow peer pressure to dictate your actions, you're no longer in the driver's seat. You *freely* hand the keys to your life over to someone else.

I know this description paints an extreme picture of a person's mindset, but it's precisely what I wanted to do — paint an extreme picture! I had a hard time accepting this, but it was necessary for me to go through it, in order for me to understand the urgency of making adjustments to my life.

Don't get the wrong impression. Peer pressure doesn't always lead to reckless behavior or things going wrong, and it shouldn't be viewed in that manner. Positive peer pressure normally yields positive results. Accomplishing things and having other people acknowledge your efforts feels great. You'll do everything you can to keep the energy flowing.

One thing I've learned is it's a better philosophy to do the right thing instead of the popular thing, because the two aren't always the same. Doing the right thing isn't always looked at with the same enthusiasm as the popular thing, although the right thing is the more valuable option, in the long-term. It's not always as exciting, because the popular things are noticed by more people. Here's why.

Our brains are wired to remember things we see that are in abundance, and things that are extreme or tragic. This is why popular things are more notorious. People usually won't remember the 100 times you did something correctly, because that's expected, but you can believe they'll remember the time you *screwed something up*, as if it happened yesterday!

This is because disastrous things burn into our memory very quickly, and stay there for a long time. Think about how many times you can recall a news story in vivid detail, years after hearing it. Why is that? It's because disaster makes a more interesting subject when re-telling a story, because of the narratives used to emphasize, or possibly exaggerate it.

I've provided an explanation of how peer pressure can affect the direction of a situation, so you should have enough knowledge to recognize this obstacle when you encounter it. It's time for you to start gaining an advantage. You must figure out why you're receiving the peer pressure. Are you sending a vibe that makes people believe you'll fold? Maybe you're displaying the traits of low self-esteem, and appear to need the acknowledgment of other people to feel accepted.

There's nothing wrong with wanting affirmation from people we know. It's one of the ways we learn if our actions are acceptable or not. However, the constant need to have it from outside sources can be dangerous. This is when you start getting the crazy challenges thrown your way, and you feel obligated to accept them, in order to gain acceptance. What you fail to realize, is the people issuing the challenges risk nothing, while you risk everything, including your dignity.

This is one of the main reasons I've stressed the importance of self-honesty so frequently throughout the book. You must be able to face situations like this without caving into the peer pressure pitfall, if you want any chance at improving. That is, if in fact you *want* to improve. You may not be ready to make adjustments yet, because you're still bound to that all-too-familiar space, your comfort zone.

I began to recognize that my behavior was creating distance between me and reality. I desperately tried to fill the void left by a failed marriage, and several disappointing relationships that followed it, with a myriad of friends. What I *really* needed was an old-fashioned honest self-assessment, more than my friends' approval.

The interesting thing about my journey through self-assessment is, once I started to see things as they were presented, a number of those so-called "friends" started fading into the background. It was no longer fun for them once I started firing back with, *"Why don't you do it?"* or *"Why are you asking me to do this foolishness?"*

Once I came into my own realization and figured out I was nothing more than a source of entertainment for them, the fun factor diminished. What they saw as an end, I saw as a beginning. I was on the road to getting better, because up to that point, I'd been content with "just getting by."

What's the message here? You don't have to be a source of entertainment to be someone's friend. The people you hang out with should know not to put you in risky or compromising situations. If a person is regularly subjecting, or goading you into foolish or reckless behavior and you can recognize it, go in the opposite direction. They have their own agenda, and not necessarily *your* best interest in mind.

If you're asked to do something that sounds ridiculous, you can't be afraid to fire back at the requester. Find out why you're being asked. You may find the reason much of this nonsense is being asked of you is because you allow it. People will treat you how you allow them to treat you. This correlates to your sense of self-worth. If you portray yourself as "less than," people will *treat* you as if you're "less than." Remember what you read in chapter 2: Your behavior sends a message to the receiver, and *always* originates in your head.

Don't get me wrong. Peer pressure can be difficult to deal with. I won't say it isn't. It was a beast for me to deal with, as I was completely engulfed by it. I caved into it more times than I care to think about, but it can be overcome.

For me, the shift occurred when I started taking stock in my own development. I drew a line in the sand and pushed my integrity to the forefront, because it's the character trait I hold in the highest regard, and the trait that will piss me off if it's questioned. Coupled with building self-confidence and focusing on self-honesty, the combination of these three aspects was exactly what I needed to turn things around.

A shift in my mindset did the trick for me, and if you decide a shift in yours will be beneficial, I'm certain you will get similar results. The moment I began to matter to me, the people who ultimately didn't matter started disappearing. At that point, I was no longer allowing myself to be controlled by deflated self-esteem, willing to risk my well-being for the sake of having someone like me. I realized that I was stronger and worth a whole lot more than that. So are you!

Here's a side note: I still speak regularly to a handful of the friends I made over those years I was handicapped by peer pressure. Their actions have let me know who my true friends are, and have always been. The others' disappearances clearly showed me where I stood with them. It's okay (now), because I know how to handle it.

Naturally you want people to like you, but if they don't, *"Oh, freakin' well!"* The world will not come to an end because a person doesn't like you! Besides, someone else liking you doesn't amount to a hill of beans if you don't like *yourself*, and your self-esteem, integrity, dignity, and decency are entirely too high of a price to pay, for somebody to like you!

The best advice I can give the person who wants to shift these odds into their favor, but find themselves face-to-face with the imbalanced obstacle of peer pressure is, *"be who you are, and learn to 'like' that person!"* If you can be, and like the person you are, I promise, the people you need to like you will find their way to you, and have no problem accepting you the way you are.

At the same time, the people you *don't* need to like you will do you a tremendous favor. When they see the direction you've chosen to go, and they're no longer fulfilled by your behavior or actions, they will freely accomplish the task of removing themselves from your life *for* you! The question you need to answer to get the ball moving is, *"Who is 'yourself?'"*

9. Validation

When you began reading this book, would you have guessed that I would be pointing out so many things that may be blocking the way of progress? Did you think I'd be making a case that nearly all of these barriers are heavily influenced by *you*? Probably not, and that's okay.

I've done an exhausting amount of research, and spent time talking with thousands of people, to arrive at the topics I've included. I'm quite certain there are many more that I haven't mentioned. I also think this is a good time to remind you of what I wrote in the first chapter: everything in this book is *not* going to apply to every reader. However, each of these topics has contributed to the deprivation of success and happiness for many people. For some (as in *my* case), more than one has been blocking their path, but here's some food for thought: the first rule in conquering an adversary is being able to recognize them. To paraphrase a military expression: *"Never fire your weapon until you've positively identified your target."*

After reading about the "disease" known as peer pressure, you may still be wondering how a person could fall into the trap so easily. In defense of those people, because I was one of them, peer pressure can be relentless. Combined with low self-esteem, it's a recipe for disaster waiting to happen. If you can't (or won't) figure out what keeps making you surrender to it, you'll continue being overpowered by it.

Legally, you're an adult at age 18, and you must take responsibility for your actions. Many people are delayed in grasping this concept. Before I decided to take a stand, peer pressure was a major distraction, because I was preoccupied with people liking me. I was willing to sacrifice my *own* identity, trying to be what I thought others wanted me to be.

There's nothing wrong with wanting to feel good. It's important to get that understood. However, when wanting to feel good becomes an unhealthy obsession, it can be potentially harmful. How? When a person believes something is missing from their life, it can cause them to value feeling good over their personal safety, and *that* creates the issues.

Is there an entity that can cause damage like this? My argument is, there *is!* The interesting thing is, like most of the topics I've discussed so far, it's created in your head, and goes hand-in-hand with peer pressure. The entity is *validation*.

Validation is the confirmation a person receives when an action or idea of theirs has been favorably received by an outside entity. This stamp of approval makes the person feel good about what they've done. In this chapter, I'll be discussing validation and the effects it can have. The idea is to highlight how not being in control of the urge for it might be what's blocking the path to success and happiness, mainly due to the lengths people have shown they're willing to go to obtain it.

I mentioned this in the chapter on haters, but the same holds true for the person constantly seeking validation. Some people are so starved for validation, that they'll ignore facts, reason, science, statistics, and logic. They'll believe, and even make up complete *nonsense*, if it makes them feel validated.

I've heard validation referred to as a "silent killer." I like this reference, for two reasons. First, you'll rarely see it coming until it's too late, because *you're* most likely the root cause. I'll explain *how* in a moment. Secondly, people either don't recognize, or simply don't care about the potential dangers of obsessing over it. Now, let's look at how a person's quest for validation can grow to an unhealthy level.

Growing up, we're nurtured by the encouragement of our parents, grandparents, other family members, and teachers. As children we seek this approval, and early on, it's perfectly normal. This is how we learn what's acceptable, or unacceptable behavior. Receiving praise feels good.

In addition to looking for other people's approval of their actions, children should be taught to look within themselves for approval. This is more valuable, and often easier to obtain than someone else's. The confusion comes when this part of the equation isn't reinforced. Then, the need to have their actions approved lingers into adulthood. The person's priorities shift. They'll still be seeking outside validation, except instead of family members, teachers, or themselves, they'll be looking to friends, co-workers, and as crazy as it may sound... even complete strangers.

Knowing someone else thinks positively about your actions feeds the ego. Issues arise when the "need" morphs into an unhealthy obsession. This is why I believe validation has gotten many people (including me) into trouble.

Trouble starts brewing when a person places a large amount of weight on another person's opinion, and not enough on their own. Many times, this is largely due to their level of respect for the other person, but it could also be due to a lack of *self*-respect. In my case, I discovered it was *both*.

Some people crave seeing, or hearing other people talk about them; either what *they* have, who they know, what they've accomplished, or how well they've done. As long as this is happening, the person feels like they're being put on a pedestal. They don't feel complete unless someone else is talking about how much they're admired, envied, or praised.

The expressions used to do this will differ, depending on where you live. In major metropolitan areas, we're fulfilled when our family and friends say things like, *"Man, you a fool for that!" "You go, girl!" "That's my boy!"* or *"Man, you did the thing!"* In affluent communities it might be, *"Man, that guy is good!"* The choice of words may differ, but the sentiment is the same: approval, justification, or acceptance of an action.

I noted earlier, there's nothing wrong with approval from others, until the need to have it becomes an unhealthy obsession. How and when do things get to that point? We want our family and friends to acknowledge and appreciate our actions, right? How can that be unhealthy?

It becomes unhealthy when a person is constantly going out of their way, trying to "one up" other people. They develop a *"look what I have"* or *"look what I did"* mentality. This can cause them to have to balance on a double-edged sword.

For example, everyone wants, or wants to be the next best thing, yet no one likes a braggart. I saw this *"look what I have"* temperament displayed regularly growing up, primarily from my grandparents' generation. I've come up with what I believe is a reasonable explanation for its prevalence. I have to assume it was born out of necessity.

Following The Great Depression of the 1930s, many families were forced to rebuild their lives with little to build from. If you were able to overcome the obstacles and help your family rebound from this economic disaster, it was a tremendous feat worth celebrating. The more people who saw you'd overcome that major adversity, the better the accomplishment felt. It made the emphatic statement that you, your family, and ultimately the community had arrived.

Unfortunately, an unfiltered version of this mentality has trickled down a few generations, and landed us where we are now. The original thought of showing how communities can rebound despite the obstacles in their way has been grossly distorted. *"We have arrived"* has now somehow morphed into *"I have arrived, but you haven't."* This straddles a thin line between approval and obsession, but some people go well beyond what's necessary for validation.

You've seen them. They're constantly talking about themselves, or posting an exhausting amount of information on social media. They need other people to know what they have, where they're going, who's hanging out with them, etc. Doing this lets everyone they associate with see how well they appear to be doing. This is likely done purely to feed the ego.

However, feeding the ego doesn't always come cheaply, and many people are willing to pay a hefty price to get from someone else, what they can get from themselves for *free*. It is at *that* moment, the never-ending hunger for another person's praise begins to complicate matters. The *need* for validation becomes the unhealthy *obsession*. If they aren't careful, this can lead to the birth of a hater. Remember them? My point is you should strive for a level of success comfortable for you, not a level you think other people believe you should be.

Think about some of the things you've seen people do to convince others they "have it together." Who has the best looking car, the latest electronic devices, the most expensive clothes, or lives in the biggest house? Who hangs out with the best looking girls or most handsome guys? Who knows which celebrities? Who's most popular? The examples can go on forever, but let's assume there are many.

In any penal institution, you'll come across people in there because of how far they were willing to *go* for validation. They engaged in activity and unfortunately ended up on the wrong side of it. They're locked up because they wanted to prove something to another person, and where *is* the other person? Hopefully, they're locked up too, but in many cases, they're free. A lot of good seeking *that* validation did!

There's nothing wrong with wanting the best, but the best for whom? Is it what's best for you, or what's best for your interpretation of what *other* people think is best for you? When all is said and done, the face you see in the mirror belongs to you, and that's the only person you need to impress. If you're spending a lot of time trying to get others to acknowledge your actions or accomplishments, you're trying to feed your ego at someone else's expense.

A person digs themselves into this predicament by using a technique I call "fishing." This is where a person regularly puts information out in the universe by whatever means, in efforts to receive attention from others. Some may try to argue with me, but I believe the constant need for attention and validation is a person's way of filling a void they believe exists, just like the group followers in Chapter 5.

I have no doubt that you've seen a post on social media that sounds similar to this: *"I need any and all prayers today. Days like this make me want to give up. I'm so sick of everything! Things are closing in, and nobody cares! Why won't anybody pick up their phone? Oh, well..."*

If you notice, there is no reference to a specific occurrence in this type of post. They just throw a random, generalized statement onto social media, and simply wait for the replies, which they will *undoubtedly* receive!

When you read something like this, the initial instinct is to contact them, to see if you can help. Most people would, and I wouldn't expect otherwise, but do you recall what you read about emotional responses? Some people get satisfaction from seeing 50 people "like" their posts, and another 30 people making comments like, *"What's going on? Call me!"* In their head, their action is validated because someone else is taking interest in whatever they're going though. See how that works?

I'm no stranger to the convenience of social media. However, it seems to have fooled many people into devaluing social intimacy. Nothing is off-limits! With some people, nearly every time information comes from them, it's *never* good: Their blood pressure is high. They have a friend or relative who is sick, in the hospital, gravely ill, or has passed away. Maybe a man or woman has done them wrong (in *their* mind), and they want everyone to know they're mad about it.

One of my general rules of thumb may help some people: *"Everybody you know... doesn't need to know, all the time!"* The problem with some people's ego is it's so shallow, one of the only ways they feel satisfied is if they're occupying another person's time or thoughts. Using social media to extract empathy from other people is strikingly similar to the tactics used by the Drama Creator.

What the person is doing is nothing more than employing the agenda advancement formula. Why not? It *works!* They want anyone listening to them to know how they feel, but they don't want to tell the whole story, up front. Giving bits and pieces of a story forces you to ask them questions. This simultaneously keeps you engaged, them in control of how the situation progresses, and feeds their ego.

The more traumatic their story sounds, the more engaged you'll most likely be. This keeps them relevant in your mind. While this is happening, you may not be as focused on your own situation. Remember the goal of the songwriter, or the outside entity trying to control you with fear? This is the same concept!

Everyone has to deal with tragedy. None of us can escape it. Tragedy isn't, nor will ever be an isolated problem. This may not sound very pleasant, but it's important for the attention-seeking, frequent social media tragedy poster to hear: *"You're not as important to other people as you think you are!"*

It's the same thing when you see someone constantly posting their relationship adventures on social media. One day, they're elated about the relationship: *"No matter what anyone says, it's you and me against the world, babe!"* Two days later, they're posting cryptic messages like, *"The hardest thing you'll ever have to endure is loving someone who doesn't want to love you back."* It's an exhausting, never-ending cycle with them. Every other day, it's either up or down.

Everything that happens to you happens for a reason. The conflict comes when you can't *accept* the reason it's happening. Is it possible that the reason you're going through these constant ups and downs is because you're being told to spend time by yourself, but have been choosing to ignore it?!

What I'm saying is ensure your *own* house is sturdy before seeking outside validation. Social media is great, but everyone doesn't need to know your business. Some things aren't for social media. Posting your drama gives people ammunition to try and break you, or keep you down. If you're constantly posting disasters and drama, people will wonder about you. Truthfully, *you* should wonder about you!

Maybe it's just me, but seeing or hearing someone constantly complaining about "catastrophic" events in their life makes me want to go in another direction. I don't have the time or energy for that negativity. Misery may need company, but it *"don't need me!"*

If this is the imbalance you're battling, you can start making your life more enjoyable by not waiting for other people to validate you. Spend some time getting to know the person you are, and develop the confidence to know that you can accomplish things by and for yourself, and be okay with that. If *you* don't think you're doing well, no one else's words are going to make you feel any differently. Validation from others is wonderful, but it isn't as necessary as you think.

If you truly have things together, your validation will come naturally. It won't be forced, where people feel *obligated* to engage with you. They'll freely engage with you because they'll feel you offer them something that enhances their life.

It's one thing for *you* to be thankful for what you have, and what you have accomplished. It's completely different when you expect *other people* to be thankful for what you have, or have accomplished! This goes back to forcing your beliefs onto another person, then getting upset if they don't accept your beliefs. I say again, everyone doesn't have to do what you do, *regardless* of what you may think.

Still craving the feeling of validation? *Look in a mirror!* The person staring back at you is the only person you need validation from. Anything above that is to feed your ego.

You are *more* than enough to satisfy the hunger for validation! The answer to whether you're doing the right thing for you is, and always *has* been… inside of you!

10. Greatness is Inside of You

Building upon the previous chapter, it's now time to start shining the spotlight on the most valuable asset you possess: *you!* Getting the full effect of this chapter is going to require active participation from you, in the form of providing responses to a couple of rhetorical scenarios. There are no right and wrong responses. The intent is to get you to conduct a conscious assessment of your current situation.

How would you react if someone told you that you have great things inside of you? Would you believe them? The majority of people would, but what if they took it a step further and told you great things are inside of you, but you haven't found a way to bring them out yet, and they may be able to help you do that? What would your reaction be, then? Would you think they were certifiably insane?

Most people would respond positively to the above scenarios, though they might be a bit hesitant with the second one. Now, here's a follow-up question. If such a large percentage of people would respond positively to these scenarios, why hasn't there been much collective progress in society? Don't worry – as I stated, these are rhetorical scenarios, but I'll offer a few responses to them.

Each person needs to find their niche. They must find the best way to make use of the gifts they were born with, because every person is born with at least one. Unfortunately, too many people interchange "gift" and "talent." They view "gift" as some sort of sports or entertainment ability, but millions of people have achieved great things in their lives without the assistance of sports or entertainment.

Here's an undeniable fact: everyone can't be the athlete, or the entertainer. Someone has to be the physician who provides treatment when the athlete or entertainer gets injured or sick. Someone must manage the financial accounts, or design the marketing strategy to create additional income. It's difficult to do these things, *and* run the football, hit the buzzer-beating shot, star in the next summer blockbuster movie, or crack the top-10 on the music charts.

Remember the question asked about why there hasn't been much collective progress? Yet again, it's the result of a perception created in a person's head. Pick any community: urban, suburban, or rural. There are people within that community waiting on cures for medical conditions. Gangs have become more prevalent. Domestic disputes and other crime rates are on the rise. Overt and covert hatred is being spewed. People are, and continue to become addicted to drugs and/or alcohol. We're battling poverty, child hunger, and veteran homelessness. Facts and statistics have confirmed that no community is immune to these types of afflictions.

Illegal (and in some cases, legal) drug use is probably the worst of these success-hampering culprits. Why? The intentional ingestion of illegal drugs is one of four things listed in the last paragraph that is completely controlled by the person. Racism, hatred, and crime are the other three.

Drugs have derailed too many lives to count. They've taken looks, intelligence, families, houses, cars, and money away from people who've chosen to use them. They've produced some of the most despicable behavior imaginable, and driven wedges between families, friends, and co-workers. They've created chaos in every community, because in many cases use turns into abuse in a short amount of time.

To me, the most infuriating about drug abuse is it's 99.9% *preventable!* Of course an addiction can develop following a medical procedure. That's not what I mean. I'm referring to the intentional consumption of illegal drugs. What's interesting is the majority of drug addicts will tell you they probably wouldn't have gotten hooked, if they'd never tried their drug of choice, in the first place.

Now, I've never taken illegal drugs and have no desire to. I can't, and won't pretend I know what it feels like to be high – I have no clue! I can only speak from what I've observed in abusers and addicts, and *"it ain't a pretty picture."*

This isn't knocking those who believe one of their pleasure sources is getting high. It may be the only thing they know. To each his or her own, but I've seen enough evidence to convince me that drugs have no useful purpose in my life. Your perception may be showing you something different.

With the amount of anti-drug campaigns, images depicted in movies and TV shows (exaggerated or otherwise), or by observing communities in nearly every city, it's reasonable to assume that the message about how drugs can absolutely *wreck* a person's life would have sunken in, by now!

197

There are hundreds of stories of people in every social status, from homeless to celebrity. Two things are certain about drugs: they have no feelings, and they do *not* discriminate!

People use illegal drugs for one reason: they want to get high… period! There's no other purpose for them. Drugs get people high, and from what I've seen, they deliver 100% of the time. I've yet to see a person use drugs without the intent of getting high. Furthermore, if they don't reach their desired high with the first use, they use more until they *do* reach it.

The question in my mind isn't whether a person wants to get high. I'm more interested in why they want to get high. There are numerous reasons, which include, but are not limited to: stress, peer pressure, trying to fit in, or social acceptance. Unfortunately, some people want to deaden the pain of a traumatic experience, and drugs are the anesthesia.

The debate over whether marijuana should be classified as a drug could probably continue forever with no resolution. As someone who has never tried drugs, I'm in no position to argue one way or the other, and I won't. The benefits and dangers of marijuana may never be fully known. It has helped some, and harmed others. I'll leave it there.

The issues *I'm* interested in reach deeper than the classification of a substance. They lend themselves to that insatiable hunger to "one up" other people. People spend a great deal of time searching for the next best drug and inventing new ways to get as high as possible, as quickly as possible. Some of these methods have proven to be extremely dangerous, yet people are still willing to try them.

I've seen people boasting on social media about how high they get, how high they got, or the potency of the drug they use. Their activity comes complete with descriptions and pictures, yet in the same breath, they'll complain about being unable to find a job, or whining about losing the job they have. They insist that the *system* keeps knocking them down.

What's usually missing is the small amount of discretion required when posting on social media. More and more employers, law enforcement, creditors, etc., are using social media as a means to find out about people's personalities, habits, and life choices. Companies even hire workers to surf the net looking for patterns in current or potential employees.

Instead, the person assigns blame to an inanimate object (the system), and label *it* as the cause of their dilemma. If an employer comes across this information, do you think they'll hire you? Keep you? My guess is likely not. As such, the person's progress is being stalled by their *own* actions.

Collectively, why haven't people made much progress? There are an infinite number of explanations for this. Ask the question multiple times and each response you get would be accurate, at least in part. Here's my take on it.

The following statement can apply to almost any scenario where a person is heading in the wrong direction, remains in a dead-end relationship, or repeatedly commit crimes, uses drugs, or engages in other activities that stifle their progress. I call it a "foot-stomp" statement, and I want you to remember it: *"Those who do not believe they deserve better, will accept and be content with what they get."*

As a recruiter for the Air Force in Arizona, I made regular visits to various high schools and colleges. I enjoyed having conversations with students, because listening to their responses to questions kept me entertained. I couldn't blame them for their responses. I'd been in high school before. I saw myself in them, and hearing them use many of the same responses I used at their age, made me laugh.

One of my favorite questions to ask was, *"What are your career plans after high school?"* I enjoyed hearing where their minds were. I kid you not... among young ladies the most popular response was, *"I want to be a nurse."* Of course I know there are male nurses, so don't get wound up. I just heard the response so often, it got me thinking: *"If this many young ladies want to be nurses, why is there a shortage of nurses all over the world?"*

The most logical answer is at some point, people figure out that they really don't want to be a nurse, for whatever reason. However, when a high school student is asked about their career plans by an Air Force recruiter, outlining a plan with a lot of details seems like a sensible response. Saying they want a career that requires a lot of college should be enough to make a recruiter be quiet, right? Not *Kevin!*

I knew the Air Force had over 200 career fields, including nurses, and several education assistance programs. So, someone telling me they needed to go to college wasn't *nearly* enough to get me to shut up, because I knew better. I developed counters for nearly every response a student could give me. I'm sure I annoyed many people, but I wanted to ensure they had facts instead of assumptions.

I also knew every student wasn't going to college immediately after high school. I was one of those who didn't. As a senior in high school, the idea of spending four more years in school was the last thing on my mind. My mom was pressuring me about attending college, but I barked right back at her. I wasn't ready to head down that road.

Additionally, I had to face the harsh, but necessary reality that I wouldn't be playing baseball for a living, as I'd envisioned at age 11. I was a good player, but nowhere close to the star on my team. So, playing baseball professionally would have been (at best) an absolute long-shot!

To further complicate matters, I missed the financial aid deadline at the college I "said" (to keep my mom quiet) I wanted to attend. Looking back, I wonder if I subconsciously but *intentionally* missed it due to my lack of enthusiasm for college? It certainly seems like a reasonable argument.

Since playing professional baseball wasn't a realistic option, and I wasn't ready to tackle college at the time, my alternative plan was the armed forces. It sounds a bit cliché-ish, but I saw it as an easy way to get out on my own, and get my mom off my back about doing something with my life. I love my parents, but I no longer wanted to live under their roof. I wanted to do things my way. I had a job, but not nearly enough money after taxes to maintain a household.

When I told my mom I planned to enlist in the armed forces, I immediately saw the concern on her face, and heard the disappointment in her voice. Being a veteran, my dad was more receptive to the idea. I think his philosophy was, *"I don't care what you do. Just do something constructive!"* Truthfully, I think he was just happy he never had to come bail me out of jail!

I remember a conversation I had with him, because I was curious about the discussions he and my mom had about me enlisting in the Air Force. I'd suspected they had some doosies. As I suspected, my mom was upset, but my dad was my chief advocate. He told her she needed to let me make my decision for me, not for *her*. He said he knew they didn't raise a dummy and was confident I'd make wise decisions. Hearing that made me feel great! Thinking back on it, at age 19, I was actually able to make a beneficial decision for myself.

Fast forward two decades and thousands of miles traveled (overseas and back), and I enjoyed the privilege of both of them sitting in the audience as I delivered a speech for my retirement from active duty. For the record, Mom and Dad both confirmed they felt I made the right decision for me. I received my validation!

Joining the Air Force may not have been the most popular decision in our household, but proved to be the path I needed to take. I'm glad the situation unfolded the way it did, because none of us had time to react to its unfolding. I received a call from my recruiter, and less than 24 hours later, I found myself at the airport headed to basic training, with literally nothing but the clothes I was wearing!

The first thing I remember seeing when I arrived was a sign that spanned the highway: *"Welcome to Lackland Air Force Base – The Gateway to the Air Force."* I was excited about the future, but terrified about venturing into an unknown world.

One thing was for certain though: I wasn't satisfied with my life as it was in Oakland. I needed something more.

Figuratively speaking, one of the biggest handicaps for teenagers is imagining any adult as a teenager. What teenagers see, adults have *seen*. I knew I wasn't the first, and wouldn't be the last person to not go to college right after high school, if at all. I knew many things could happen between, *"I graduated from high school"* and *"I'm a successful adult."*

My goal in recruiting was simple: provide people with alternatives to look at, in case their Plan A didn't work out as planned. Naturally I wanted everyone I talked with to join the Air Force, but for one reason or another, they all couldn't. To make my point, I'll share the stories of two young men.

The first young man was a model student. School was easy for him, and he graduated as class valedictorian. Prior to that, I'd asked him about his post-high school plans. Mind you, it was a no-pressure situation. He said he was "all set." He had (as he put it) a *"full-ride to U of A"* (The University of Arizona) and didn't *"need to hear anything about the Air Force."*

Let me repeat that, so you get the full effect of what I'm saying. I asked him about his plans after high school, and his reply was, he didn't need to hear anything about the *Air Force*. I hadn't mentioned the Air Force to him, yet his reply was based on an assumption *he* created. See how that worked?

Of course, I couldn't blame him. After all, I *was* wearing an Air Force uniform, and my job *was* recruiting. I made similar assumptions about recruiters when I was in high school. I felt none of them had anything I wanted or needed, so I avoided them, as he was doing to me. Each time I visited the school following that, he avoided me like the plague.

I'd gotten used to students ducking me at nearly every school I visited, but this young man took it to an extreme. He even tried to avoid making eye contact with me! What did he think I was going to do? Club him over the head and throw him on a bus to basic training? Did he think I knew some hidden hypnosis trick? Perhaps he felt intimidated, because I didn't fit his perception of the "typical" military recruiter.

Following his graduation, I didn't think much about him. About six months later, I went through a drive-thru for lunch. Take a wild guess who handed my food to me when I got to the window?! None other than *Mr. Valedictorian!*

I recognized him immediately, and I'm quite certain he recognized me. I was in uniform, and the sole Air Force recruiter within a 70-mile radius. He tried to keep our encounter as professional as he could. I did as well… *almost!*

Being the smart aleck I am, I wanted to rub it in a little. He wouldn't give me the time of day when he was in high school, and I was only trying to help him. He was about to learn *that* day!

How did I drive my point home? I asked him for extra ketchup! When he gave it to me, I politely smiled, thanked him by name, and started driving away. The look on his face was *priceless!* That small token victory was mine and he knew it. Yes, I was being petty – I'll *own* that!

I found out later while talking to one of his friends that things at the U of A started out well for him. Unfortunately, he soon found out the hard way that no one is going to hold your hand in college. He started missing classes, his grades dropped, his scholarship was rescinded, and back he came. He was back in the same small city he tried so hard to get away from in the first place, working at a fast-food restaurant.

There's nothing wrong with the fast-food industry. Some awesome people work in it. However, this had to be a tremendous blow to the young man's overly-inflated ego, considering the status he'd achieved in high school. Had he taken time to speak with me, he may have been able to look at other alternatives. I sincerely hope he found his niche.

The second young man was the star athlete. Every week I'd open the newspaper and there was his name and picture. I struck up a conversation with him while visiting his school. I wanted to talk with him because of his influence on other students. I noticed strong leadership qualities in him.

With each person I had the opportunity to speak with, my message was the same: *"Have a backup plan, in case career plan A doesn't work out the way you want it to."* I knew this, because *my* plan A didn't work out the way I'd planned. As you could expect, "Mr. Athlete's" attitude was similar to "Mr. Valedictorian's." He made it a point to tell me in no uncertain terms that he had a full-ride scholarship, and didn't need a backup plan. I'm sure you can see where this is headed.

As many high school students do, this young man made the crucial mistake of thinking with a one-track mind. He brushed aside what I was saying because it contradicted *his* thinking. Unfortunately for him, he fell victim to his own hype, and failed to understand the conditions of a sports scholarship. It can be rescinded as fast as it was awarded, if the recipient no longer fulfills the criteria for the scholarship. Nowhere is this truer than with sports scholarships, because anything can, and often does happen. Of course, my words fell on the deaf ears of a teenaged star athlete who believed he was invincible.

Sure enough, life threw a curveball to someone who was looking for a *fastball!* The young man suffered a horrific injury. Due to its severity, the university he planned to attend felt he was no longer worth their investment, and rescinded his scholarship before he stepped foot on campus. Was that fair? It's a matter of opinion. If the university was looking for him to play a particular sport, but he couldn't perform to their expectations, it may have been within its rights to do so.

I felt bad for him, because I'm certain he could have become a professional athlete. Here's a side note: despite my references to describe his situation, he did *not* play baseball, and I was pleased to learn he accepted a partial scholarship to a junior college. It wasn't the full-ride to a Division I school he anticipated, but it *was* a way for him to play the sport he loved. More importantly, he could advance his education.

Both these young men learned the hard way, when you're planning for a career, you must be prepared for the unexpected, and not put all your eggs in one basket. They were blinded by their ambition, and felt I had nothing substantial to offer them. Who knows where they would have ended up if they'd explored more than just their top option?

I'm not relishing in either young man's misfortune, though I have to admit, I took a small amount of solace with Mr. Valedictorian. The look of absolute befuddlement on his face had me smiling all the way back to the office!

I remember my dad saying: *"Don't turn down an opportunity, simply because it doesn't come wrapped the way you want it."* Often, we look for the package with the colorful wrapping paper, strings, and bows, when in reality, the package wrapped in the plain brown paper is identical, and *will* suffice. It isn't about how the package is wrapped, but what's inside.

My time as a recruiter helped me develop an important characteristic: *tenacity*. Hearing certain things repeatedly makes you adjust, so you don't drive yourself insane while doing your job. Hearing *"no"* a lot forced me to alter my tactics, in hopes of not hearing *no* as much, and getting some *yeses* sprinkled here and there. Fortunately for me, I heard *yes* more than *no* among people who took time to speak with me.

I also came to a realization that many people are disillusioned about their ability. This means they tend to sell themselves short. Therefore, they refuse to allow themselves to fully develop. I'll say it, again: *"Those who don't believe they deserve better, will accept and be content with what they get."*

The paralyzed (there's that word, again!) person doesn't believe they have the ability to find a cure for cancer. They don't see themselves as an anti-drug campaign advocate. They can't see themselves making a difference because in their mind, they're one person. One person can't make a difference, right? *Wrong!* Sometimes, one person makes the only difference needed! Read the following example:

A man was imprisoned for nearly three decades, for challenging laws in his country that he saw as oppressive and unfair. During his incarceration, he was subjected to unbelievable punishment, ridicule, and torture. Through all of this, he never wavered in his opposition to the legislation. He believed that one day those unjust laws would be rescinded.

He stood fast in his beliefs, in the face of adversity. He dared to defy an entire country's legislation, and refused to let even imprisonment break his spirit and drive. He never backed down, and continued his opposition to these laws following his release. He became a major catalyst in challenging the laws which imprisoned him. Fast forward a few years, and the man who was once a political prisoner was elected *president!* How about *that* for making a difference?

I'm speaking of course, of the former president of South Africa, the late Mr. Nelson Mandala (PBS, 1995). He was probably the major champion in toppling South Africa's apartheid law. What he accomplished is a terrific example of how determination is the trait needed to push a person to achieve a goal they've set. He was one man with the courage to challenge an entire government, and in the end… it was the government that shifted *its* position!

I'm not sure when Mr. Mandala set his sights on becoming President of South Africa, but his decision to do so is the perfect example to illustrate that you should never limit yourself. You don't know what you can accomplish until you have to go beyond the limits you've established in your mind. Whether you believe it, know it, or not, greatness is inside you! You need to tap into that greatness, and a good start to trying to do that, is by establishing some goals.

I said before, saying and doing are two different things. Many people stop at stating their goal, but you'll have to go a lot further if you want to achieve it. I suggest writing it down. This provides a written record you can refer to when you get sidetracked, which will happen from time to time, in the beginning. It will occur less and less as you become more focused on your goals, and make progress toward it.

I'll paraphrase an absolutely brilliant quote I heard once, though I can't find the source after researching exhaustively. Who said it isn't as important as what was said, but I think it packs a powerful punch: *"Set a goal so big, the only way you can achieve it is to grow into the person who can!"*

When setting goals, I use the "S.M.A.R.T." approach (Meyer, 2003). This is an acronym of five characteristics that must be present for a goal to be effective. Many people don't pay enough attention to this when setting their goals, and end up giving up on the goal much sooner than they should.

The elements in S.M.A.R.T. are: Specific, Measureable, Attainable, Realistic, and Time-Sensitive. Every goal you set should encompass all of the elements. The step many people miss, if they even *get* to this point, is acknowledging and embracing the actions necessary to achieve their goal.

As mentioned with other topics we've discussed, you must be prepared for the unexpected. What's required or necessary to achieve your goal may be actions you don't *want* to do, or even *like* doing. However, if you're going to achieve the goal, you *need* to do them. I was taught, *"You don't have to like it. You just have to do it!"* In other words, enjoy the *destination*, not the journey you had to take to get there.

Metaphorically speaking, each of us is born with a blank canvas. The canvas is ours to decorate as we see fit. We receive materials in the form of information and experience, and we use what we feel helps us decorate our canvas. However, what we *feel* is best and what *is* best may differ.

How many times have you, or someone you know made a decision, only to discover it was the wrong decision? If you answered *"never,"* you're telling one of those dangerous lies. You may have bigger issues, because you haven't learned, and continue to underestimate what I've been highlighting throughout this book: the importance of self-honesty!

The fact is we've all done it. You can't learn if things have never gone wrong. The idea is to learn from mistakes. This is how knowledge is gained. However, there is a fine line between making a mistake, and looking like a jackass.

The person who makes a mistake acknowledges the mistake, and adjusts their behavior to avoid making the mistake again. The jackass makes a mistake, *realizes* it's a mistake, but continues the action! The latter is why so many people recycle through the criminal justice system.

Let's say a person is in jail for theft, for the tenth time. Of course, stealing is illegal almost everywhere, and has been for about... *ever!* I don't see it changing anytime in the foreseeable future. If you're caught stealing, you're going to jail... *period*. Our criminal has been caught 10 times. How can he possibly think he's doing things correctly?!

Oh wait, I get it! On that tenth time, stealing was going to miraculously become legal, because police departments will have grown tired of arresting people for it. Yep... it sounds stupid when I say it, too!

For the record, I'm not calling everyone who engages in criminal activity a jackass! Nor do I believe anyone sets out to become a career criminal. Many have been lured into crime by the excitement. Quick money, possessions, getting over, and coming by things the *"easy way"* are attractive by-products when you don't *have*, but you *want*. Others are forced into it for survival. In survival mode, you'll do what you feel is necessary to fulfill the needs you have.

If you're contemplating crime as your path to prosperity, you need to also consider the following: criminal activity *rarely* results in a long, peaceful life. You can expect a lot of turmoil if you choose to engage in these activities over a long period. The chances are much greater that you'll get caught, than get away. What you'll be doing is taking a gamble with your life. It's a gamble where the odds are largely stacked against you, and there aren't many ways to shift those odds to your favor. Do you continue down that path, though you *know* it usually doesn't end in a good place? Alarmingly, a number of people *will!*

When things don't go as planned, the thing to do is take a step back and analyze what happened. See where things went awry, regroup, and revise your plan. You can make a mistake once. If you try an action a second time and get the same result as the first, it's not a *mistake.* You made a *choice!*

Perhaps an alternative offered before he committed his first crime could have prevented our criminal from heading down that path, in the first place. Someone influential in his life could have explained to him that crime, in its basic form, is 100% *preventable!* They could have shown him other methods of obtaining the items he desired that didn't involve resorting to participating in criminal activities.

My point, is how many times do things have to go wrong, before you change your method of operation? In our criminal's case, things went wrong 10 times, yet he continued his behavior as if anticipating a different result. He wasn't caught stealing 10 times by chance. He was caught because he decided to continue stealing. That's *choice…* not *chance!*

He chose to ignore the pre-determined consequences associated with stealing, and it led him right to where he's sitting. He failed to realize that while he voluntarily dictated the direction of the action, he had no control over the *reaction.* He couldn't have predicted the end result, and that's the point. Getting away was his plan, but he was caught. Now, he's an involuntary participant in the *prison system's* plan.

Although my criminal is fictional, people regularly face dilemmas like these. He was held back because of his perception. He'd convinced himself that crime was his best (and probably *only*) option. In *his* mind, the *possibility* of gaining prosperity by engaging in criminal activity outweighed the *probability* of incarceration. He adversely impacted his situation with behavior he developed in his own head!

The same can be said of people who remain in dead-end relationships, or continue using drugs. They've convinced themselves that their current option is their *best* option. They've deliberately undersold themselves because they don't believe they deserve better. I've mentioned self-sabotage a few times now, and these are all further illustrations of it.

Every person is capable of achieving greatness. It's because "greatness" is largely subjective, and can mean different things to different people. The key is tapping into that greatness before negative influences overtake the positive ones. The sooner you learn how to do this, the better your chances are of making a beneficial decision.

You can shift these odds into your favor by learning to stop doubting your ability, and start utilizing your gifts! You have greatness inside of you. The question is, *"Are you prepared for that greatness to surface?"* If you say you're prepared, you better make certain you *are*, because if you plan to implement some of things I'm suggesting in this book, be prepared, because your journey is about to make a dramatic shift, and it's going to happen, quickly!

Start by setting your goals using the S.M.A.R.T. concept. Break each goal into small "sub" goals. Not doing this will make it difficult to recognize actual progress toward the goal, and easy to be discouraged about not achieving it.

"I want to lose 15 pounds" sounds great on the surface, but it's too broad to be effective. *"I want to lose 15 pounds over the next 2 months"* doesn't sound like it's much different, but it hits *every one* of the S.M.A.R.T. characteristics. The only thing left is to outline how you're going to achieve it. Shift your mindset and put your focus and efforts on the goal, and be willing to do what's necessary. For my example, to lose weight, you must burn more calories than you consume… period! What may be necessary is altering the way you eat, and regular exercise. There's no other natural way to do it.

Finally, regarding shortcuts. They only yield short-term results. If your shortcut fails, you must start again, and find another way to get over the obstacle, which essentially *doubles* your workload. Take our fictional criminal as an example.

What do you plan to do with the information you've been reading in this book? Use it? Share it? Think about this a second: if everyone tapped into their ability, and capitalized on what they're good at, the world would be in better shape. If you can focus on your strengths, and embrace your weaknesses, the weaknesses won't be weaknesses, very long!

I'm reminded of something my grandfather said to me once: *"When you think you're down and out, and feel like you want to give up, remember this — the toughest battles are only given to the strongest soldiers!"*

11. Facing and Overcoming Obstacles

Is your head spinning, yet? I said I would challenge your thinking in some unconventional ways, right? I've identified several topics that may be creating detours on your journey to success and happiness. I'll remind you of what you read in the "Finding You" chapter: *"Where you are, is exactly where you're supposed to be,"* and in the Comfort Zone chapter: *"You didn't get to where you are, by accident."* The decisions you've made thus far, have gotten you to where you are.

Regardless of the decisions that got you *to* this point, what's important are the decisions you make *from* this point. What's your next move? Maybe you like your situation. If so, great, but if not, do you continue allowing the circumstances to conquer you, and accept the status quo as destiny? Or do you devise a plan to create a situation more to your liking? You've come to a fork in the road. Which path do you take?

Each path has a set of consequences associated with taking it. Earlier, I said every encounter will teach you, or reinforce what you should do, or should not do. The decisions you make based on your interpretation of these encounters will determine if you chose the correct path.

If your life hasn't unfolded as you've planned, it's likely because you haven't overcome the majority of the obstacles that have been in your way. Perhaps you don't recognize them, but there's also a chance that you *do* recognize them, but for whatever reason, have chosen not to negotiate them. You may feel you aren't equipped to handle them, and have accepted them as par for the course. Regardless of the reason, not much progress has been made, and it's frustrating. I know exactly how that feels. I've been there.

The thing to remember is on your journey through life, you'll encounter obstacles that may or may not be unique to you, whether they're physical or mental. The mental obstacles are generally tougher to overcome, because they don't originate from someone else. It might sound strange, but it could be *you* putting the obstacles in the way, and impeding your progress, using little more than your own brainpower!

The road to success, while paved, has off-ramps at different junctions in route to the finish line (the goal). Some of those off-ramps are positive, while others are negative. No one has ever been promised an easy road to success. If it were easy, everyone would be taking it! The road is long and windy, but well worth the journey when you have the tools to prepare for it.

As mentioned earlier, the only defense you can muster to help you through these challenges is preparedness. Being prepared at least puts you in a frame of mind where you'll want to find ways to overcome the challenges as you encounter them. Here's another one of those foot-stomp statements you may want to burn into the old memory bank: *"One of the most difficult challenges you will ever face, is a challenge from an outside entity to change something you've grown comfortable doing."*

There have been studies conducted that suggest it takes 21 days to break a habit. I'd argue while physically it may take 21 days, mentally it can take much longer. It depends on the amount of emotional weight you've assigned to the activity or behavior, and how long you've been doing it. The longer you've done something, the more mentally invested you are. As such, you're not as eager to dismiss it.

For example, everyone has a favorite food. It's almost impossible to dismiss that food quickly if you've been eating and enjoying it for a long time. Admittedly, mine is barbeque. Not eating barbeque for 21 days wouldn't be an issue. The issue would be mentally getting over the taste of barbeque. I've assigned an enormous amount of emotional weight to it, so the memory created by the taste of barbeque would take much longer than 21 days to get over. I guarantee it!

The way I describe my adoration for barbeque is similar to what many people do when they encounter obstacles. They unintentionally (or maybe intentionally) make the obstacle larger than it really is. When an obstacle appears too large to handle, a person can mentally defeat themselves before making an attempt to negotiate it. It gets filed under the *"I can't…"* category in their head, and is another example of how a person's own brainpower can block their path to success and happiness.

Obstacles are nothing new, and they aren't going anywhere. Get used to dealing with them. They're part of the personal growth process. When you're striving to gain something meaningful, obstacles are going to be in the way, to try and discourage you. It's up to you to respond to them in a way that's beneficial to you.

You must be on the lookout for nay-sayers and dream killers, because they can be as big of an obstacle as a physical barrier. These are the people who tell you can't do something, or what you want to accomplish is impossible, or a bad idea. Tell them your goal, and the first thing they do is start giving you a bunch of reasons why you shouldn't do it, or why they think your goal is a "bad idea." What I want you to remind yourself of is, the nay-sayer's actions only create the circumstances. *You* decide if those circumstances pack enough punch to persuade you to not pursue the goal.

Nay-sayers will come along and freely give you their philosophy, as soon they notice you've decided to start improving your life, even if you didn't *ask* them for it. Why? *"Misery needs company!"* The question is, *"On whose philosophy will you place the most value?"* Surely the correct answer is yours, but you've read numerous examples where I've pointed out people who have unwittingly chosen the other person's.

The amount of effort is what separates good and great. Anyone can be good, but with a bit more effort, the greatness that's been lying dormant inside you can rise to the surface. Don't know how to start tackling the obstacles? Well, that's the easy part! You tackle them the same way they were introduced to you – one at a time! You can only truly focus on one thing at a time. Analyze the obstacles, prioritize them, and line them up in your preferred order. Then, get to work knocking them down in the exact order you lined them up!

Adopting this mentality makes perfect sense. Many people already know it, or may have finished reading it only a few seconds ago, yet they will *still* try to tackle everything at once! If you do this, you'll continue feeling frustrated, overwhelmed, and discouraged, and I don't want you to feel that way. Allow me to share a personal example of how pushing passed obstacles pays off.

I was working in the Air Force as a healthcare recruiter. At the beginning of each year, recruiting goals are distributed. One particular year, the goals were ridiculously high. They were intentionally increased by nearly 900% over the previous year, to justify a request for an increase in personnel. The "powers that be" were making a point to the powers that be above them, and using the recruiters in the field as leverage. There was little chance of many recruiters achieving their assigned goal, and everyone except the top decision makers knew it.

Many of my counterparts immediately revolted. I talked to several around the country and the sentiment was basically the same: *"Man, I'm not even trying to make my goal! There's no way I'm going to be able to find* _____ (insert an insanely large number and a healthcare specialty)."

I took a decidedly different approach. I saw the goals like everyone else, but something in my head told me if that many people weren't even making an effort to achieve their goal, there was a larger market of candidates for me to work with, and I could use it to my advantage. Blame that on my *"drink it and eliminate the issue"* attitude.

Despite the long odds, I made the decision to step out of my comfort zone, and take a shot at the impossible. I thought, *"What's the worst that could happen? I won't make my goal? So what?! Nobody expects me to make it anyway, so there's no big loss if I don't make it."* I decided to go for it. With *that* mindset, you'd probably guess I racked up, right?

Wrong! I failed miserably! I fell well short of my goal, but an interesting thing occurred in the midst of that failure. Remember, I didn't take the same approach as everyone else. As a result, I missed my goal, but in the process, I put myself *ahead* of everyone who didn't try! I took action that separated me from the pack, and when all was said and done, I was among a handful of recruiters who received national recognition for their performance that year, though mathematically, I fell short of the expectation.

The point is an obstacle can appear insurmountable, but your perception of it makes the difference. You can't allow an obstacle's appearance scare you away from attacking it, if it's blocking the path to your goal. Perceiving the goals as my counterparts did wouldn't have gotten me recognized. I was willing to go against the grain. Thanks, Mom and Dad!

My temperament developed over time, and by and large, the people who've motivated me the most have been the nay-sayers. I don't know what it is; for me, a wild sense of satisfaction comes from proving a nay-sayer wrong! The look on their face as they watch me succeed at something they said I couldn't do is extremely gratifying.

My goals are my goals. Anyone attempting to interfere with me achieving a goal I've set only gives me an extra push. When I have my sights set on a goal, there's not much another person can do to deter me. Succeeding in spite of attempted sabotage by the nay-sayer is my way of rubbing it in their face for doubting my ability, persistence, and will.

If you want to jumpstart your transformation, I suggest adopting this philosophy because as I stated a couple of pages back, once you make the decision to start improving your life and pursue your goals, nay-sayers are going to start coming out of the woodwork like cockroaches! You can bank on it, especially if your goal contradicts what society (or maybe the nay-sayer) deems as viable.

No one… and I mean *no one* has the right to tell you how to live your life, or that what you want to accomplish with your life is wrong! If you want something, do your research, create a plan and get after it! It's that simple!

No one else can tell you what's going to satisfy you. They can only tell you what's going to satisfy *them*, and *that's* only if they've firmly defined their criteria! Here's another interesting thing about nay-sayers: they may be discouraging you from pursuing your goals, because they've decided to stop pursuing their own goals, and don't want to be left behind. Yes indeed… there's that misery thing, again!

Make a plan and start pursuing every one of your goals and dreams, because achieving them is going to make you feel great! As far as the nay-sayer is concerned, they can put super glue on the seat of their pants, and sit down somewhere!

"What about obstacles?" What *about* them? An obstacle's function is to make the journey memorable. Stay focused on the goal. Once you've overcome the obstacle and achieved the goal, the tale of your journey and subsequent triumph is something you'll gladly share with the nay-sayer, and anybody else who asks you.

When you're explaining how you persevered despite the obstacles in the way, you can internally rejoice as you watch the nay-sayer's perspective change. They'll say things like they *"knew you could do it all along!"* In your mind, you'll know the thing they did was provide you with that needed push.

Pursuing your dreams and goals is a battle of mind over matter, and should _never_ be done on someone else's schedule! Your determination to accomplish the goal must be more powerful than the obstacle's ability to defeat you. It's okay to anticipate obstacles, but you don't need to constantly stress over them. Why not? Challenges and obstacles are only as large as you make them in your head, and unless I've been mistaken my entire life, you're in complete control of your own head! I'll repeat what I wrote in the Fear of Winning chapter: *"Sometimes, the only obstacle you need to overcome is _you_!"*

Be mindful of the things you store in your head, but more importantly, be mindful of how you *process* the things you store in your head. Remember the "Drama Creator?" They *thrive* on finding things wrong! They regularly over-inflate ordinary situations, react to things that aren't there, and focus on negative aspects – *anything* to be upset about.

There is a correct and incorrect decision for every scenario, but every correct decision has a long, and a short way of achieving the desired result. Do not mistake the short *way* for a short*cut*. There is an enormous difference between these two things.

Your dreams and goals are waiting for you, but what are you doing to get you closer to achieving them? If you say you "can't," then you never will! However, if you say *"maybe,"* you give yourself a chance you wouldn't have taken otherwise.

No obstacle is too large to overcome, once you're willing to do what's necessary to overcome it. Again, I must stress that you may not want to do, or even *like* doing what you find necessary, but unless you *do* it, the obstacle will remain right where it is: *in your way!* The worst part is… you'll be *allowing* it to remain there! In case you weren't paying attention earlier, here's a textbook example of self-sabotage.

Here's something you'll want to burn *this* into your memory bank: This is your life! If the nay-sayer wants to waste theirs, go ahead and *let them!* Your task is to keep moving forward, full-steam ahead. In the long run, you'll be better off. If a nay-sayer says your goal is impossible, they're saying it's impossible for *them*. A nay-sayer *does* not… *cannot*… and should not *ever* speak for you!

In order to improve at sports, or anything else in life, you must first issue the challenge to yourself *to* improve. Then, you must develop the confidence to know you *can* improve. Finally, you have to be able to muster the courage to do what you need (not want) to do, to make it happen, even if it means reaching out to someone else for assistance. It's okay to ask for help. It's certainly more comfortable to fix things on your own, but as I stated in the first chapter, if you refuse to acknowledge something's broken, you can't fix it.

How can this approach be detrimental for you? The point I'm trying to make is… it *can't!* Even if you come up short in achieving your goal, by simply challenging yourself to become better, and knowing you can be, you'll put yourself in a better position than you were when you started. How is that? It's because once again, you'll be taking steps to overcome the most difficult obstacle you face… *you!*

I'll sum this chapter up with a basketball analogy, but use a quote from a professional hockey legend to facilitate it. Wayne Gretsky said, *"You will miss 100% of the shots you never take!"* You've been given the ball, with a clear look at the basket. Are you going to stand there holding the ball?! You'll never know if you can make the shot, if you don't take it. So… set your feet, bend your knees, lift the ball, and *shoot the damned thing!*

Of course, you may miss the shot, but if you shoot and miss, at the very least, you'll have an idea of what to work on before taking another shot. Now, consider this: what if you shoot the ball, and *"SWISH…"* it goes right through the hoop and hits nothing but the bottom of the net?! What in the world would you have wasted your time worrying about? *Nothing!* Why? Because as it turned out, you already possessed what was needed to accomplish the task in the first place!

12. Shift the Odds by Shifting Your Mindset

Congratulations! You've arrived at the last chapter of the book. After this, you can finally get off this crazy ride. I have to commend you for making to this point. The topics I've discussed haven't been the most comfortable to read, I'm sure. Nonetheless, I have confidence that many of them can help you get on, or get *back* on the path to improvement.

I must also tip my hat to you for enduring my babbling for this long! I can be long-winded, and have strong opinions about some things. My goal was to ensure the intended messages weren't lost in translation, going from the eye to the brain. It was important to me that I make a lasting, and hopefully favorable impression on you as a reader. Only you have the answer to whether I've accomplished that or not.

You've read many examples of how different our lives can be, because of the decisions and choices we make. Your chosen course will have major implications on a situation's outcome. Whether the outcome is positive or negative is often determined by a decision that is made in a split-second.

My overall intent was to highlight our similarities. I wanted to show while outward appearances can differ, people really aren't that different from each other. We're only as different as our minds make us. Many of the inner struggles we face are fairly common, regardless of your background.

Collectively, we've experienced many things though our perceptions of those things may differ. I wanted to eliminate the *"it's just me"* sentiments by giving several examples that illustrate *"it ain't just you!"*

Most people want a life where they can have the things they desire, and live comfortably. This may mean buying material things, going on vacations, or having time to engage in activities they enjoy. People want to live as stress-free of a life as possible. Well, except for the *Drama Creator*. Drama is their staple, so they need other people entangled in it, in order to maintain their desired level of comfort.

Everyone has contributed to the chaos in their life on some level through some bone-headed decision, or action. Most are able to recover, but some aren't, and that's what this chapter is intended to straighten out. Looking back on my own experiences, I can now recognize much of the drama I encountered, may have easily been avoided by me making a different decision. Hindsight is always 20/20.

In a twisted, but meaningful way, I'm thankful for the drama I've experienced. Without it, I wouldn't be the person I am. I've learned many lessons going through what I went through, at the time I went through it. Once I learned to stop creating drama, the tide of my life began to shift. Explaining how I managed to bring about these changes is what I'm attempting to accomplish with this chapter.

For the majority of people, there comes a point when the chaos and drama is too much, and the need for change is apparent. Issues arise when the person realizes changes are needed, but doesn't know how, or where to start. They may be afraid of the changes, because they've gotten comfortable with things as they are. They're stuck in their comfort zone.

I've tried to discredit as many of the generally-accepted actions that may be preventing you from breaking away from your comfort zone as I could. I wanted to help you develop the courage to step toward success, by explaining how I overcame many of my own obstacles. Perhaps you've stumbled across an idea, phrase, sentence, or entire chapter that motivates you to make a needed adjustment.

Don't make the same mistake I made, and allow the idea of change or improvement intimidate you into accepting complacency. There's a strong possibility that one of those changes you're afraid of, will result in reaching a goal you've set. Make that possibility enough to get you moving, and you've taken the first step in progressing forward. The alternative is remaining in your current rut, and perpetuating the cycle of disappointment. My family said it best: *"To achieve something different, you have to do something different."*

Success doesn't always have to translate to having a ton of money in the bank, despite what many people have conditioned themselves to believe. I've provided examples that contradict that philosophy. People have had money but still weren't fulfilled. Something was missing from their lives, and the circumstances presented were too much to shoulder. Don't forget about the people who met a premature demise by chasing money. Money helps alleviate many issues, but it's not the end all! In fact, it can *create* as many as it alleviates!

For some people, success means overcoming an obstacle they'd previously been afraid to challenge. It may be a small victory, but victories accumulated over smaller obstacles helps you build the confidence needed to take on *larger* obstacles without fear. Then, larger obstacles appear smaller, because your mindset will be in a mode where few things can deter you from pushing toward a goal.

To achieve this, an improvement plan is both logical and necessary. An updated you requires an updated plan. I've provided the blueprint and framework. It's up to you to comprehend the information and execute a workable plan.

It's time to show you how to shift the odds into your favor, so you can stop "blindly gambling" on improving your life. The first step is the same one I mentioned in the first chapter: acknowledge the aspect you're dissatisfied with. You must give it an identity. This makes it easier to isolate and form a plan to adjust, improve, or eliminate it. This gives you an identified target to launch an attack. You can't overcome an obstacle if you refuse to acknowledge its presence.

The next step is to initiate a shift in your mindset. In case every behavior pattern reference I've made thus far has gone over your head (which I seriously doubt!), I'll reveal it in plain English: *Nearly everything blocking your path to a successful and enjoyable life up to this point, has been created, or developed in your own head!*

If I can get you to subscribe to this theory, you'll be well on the way to a turnaround. In addition to that, you need to learn to step (and stay) out your own way. I've emphasized perception throughout the book, and how your reactions to the presented circumstances have contributed to your current situation, on numerous occasions. If you can believe that you've likely had a hand in *creating* your situation, then you can also believe that you have the power to *alter* it!

Shifting your mindset is the easiest, yet most difficult part of the improvement process. It's easy because the only required action is for you to make the decision to take a different course. It's difficult because your brain has been conditioned to justify your current comfort level.

There is an effective technique to aid in the mindset shift: become sick of the aspect you've identified. I mean, you need to become so sick of it, that the thought of continuing with it makes you want to *throw up!* I've said many times in this book to keep your emotions as far away from your decision-making as possible. This is *not* one of those times! In this instance, you have complete autonomy to react as emotionally as you like. Assign as much emotional weight as it takes for you to become *emphatically* sick of that aspect. I phrased it this way because if you're not emphatically sick of it, you won't be ready, or willing to do *whatever* is necessary to change it. What I'm trying to get you do is establish your *own* rock bottom. That way, the only direction to go is up!

I mentioned losing weight earlier. There are people who say they want to lose weight. You've seen them on television, or maybe it's someone you know personally. Some of them completely break down when discussing their weight issues, and look extremely depressed when they do. You feel for them, until you notice as they're pouring out their sentiments, they're also shoving a doughnut into their mouth!

This person hasn't become sick enough of the aspect to prompt a change in their thought pattern. Their health or appearance hasn't gotten on their nerves enough to motivate them to do anything different than what they're currently doing. At the moment, the taste of the doughnut outweighs the idea of weight loss, because of their perception.

Then there's the criminal who swears the last time he went to jail will be his last. There's no way he's going back. As he's saying this, he's driving with a suspended license, he's been drinking, he smells like marijuana, and his friend has more marijuana *and* a weapon under the passenger seat.

This person too, hasn't become sick enough of their circumstances to prompt a change in their behavior. The culprit again, is perception. He's convinced his activity or who he's hanging with won't cause him to go back to jail. Can you see how easily your mind can manipulate a situation?

There are dozens of examples, but let's say you've reached your tipping point, and feel it's time for a change. You're aware of your shortcomings and willing to take ownership of them, because you understand their effects they've had on you. Following this breakthrough, you'll need to conduct an honest self-assessment to recognize what you can and can't do. It's acceptable to admit you can't do certain things, because you won't do everything impeccably in *every* situation.

This is where many people tend to drop the ball. For whatever reason, they're afraid to admit they've come up short in an aspect of their lives. I can relate to this sentiment because I was one of those people. Accepting I wasn't as adept at some things as I thought was, was one of the hardest things I've had to do. Trust me, you're not alone!

Admitting shortcomings does *not* mean you're a loser who'll never make positive progress. In fact, it's quite the opposite. However, many peoples' egos are so fragile, that the possibility of failing is terrifying! They don't believe they can recover from failure. Therefore, they choose to ignore the possibility of it, as if that will make it not exist. Big mistake!

Take it from someone who has been there before: you can recover! The person who thinks they can't recover from failure normally uses evasion as a defense mechanism to shield them from reality. They choose to live in the fabricated world where they've convinced themselves that they have everything under control, when in reality, they should be telling themselves that they could use some assistance. See? Arrogance *is* often used as a mask for insecurity.

If each person had everything figured out, the world would be in a much better state. Everything would be getting better, but everything *isn't* getting better. Truthfully, many things are getting worse. Not to fear. The thing *you* need is a handle on *your* life. *"Change happens, one person at a time."*

You may have several aspects you want to improve. Determining you need to change your life in order to improve it is a frightening discovery. I've been there, and it's not fun! I realized I needed to make numerous changes, but had no clue where to start. Here's the wonderful thing I discovered about making multiple changes: you don't have to make all the changes at once. Allow me to share my life improvement theory.

One of the most important keys to improvement is the employment of *balance*. I've referenced it in numerous places in the book, and it's finally time to show you its importance. It took me a while to figure it out. I took a lot of bumps on the head before it finally clicked, but when it did, I was able to nail down what I've deemed my ideal formula for achieving success and happiness in life. My formula consists of only four elements, but it is *essential* to succeeding at any task. It has helped me straighten out my previously-chaotic life, and I'm confident it will help you, as well.

I've developed an acronym to make the formula easy to remember: *"DOME."* The amazing thing is it can be applied to 99.9% of situations. When it's applied effectively, the end result should be positive for the person applying it. Before I break the formula down, I want to examine the basic definition of the acronym to frame my perspective.

In its basic context, when a person hears the word *dome*, the image that normally comes to mind is a stadium, or some sort of confined space with a top on it. Underneath the top is a restricted amount of space, which gives the impression that space is limited.

I see *dome* quite differently. I see it as the key to unlocking your potential, if you accept my explanation. If you apply the formula to your life, it will reveal paths to improvements you may have thought were unattainable. It's difficult to mess up once you've mastered the concept. It'll take time getting accustomed to using it regularly, but once it's been ingrained in your mind, it's there permanently.

A few paragraphs ago, I made a statement that one of the keys to succeeding at life's tasks is balance. If you can apply the elements of the DOME formula in balance with each other, there's no way you should fail at any task you attempt. With that, let's examine the formula's elements.

The first letter in the word DOME is of course, D. It stands for *desire*. It's the amount of energy a person is willing to spend to achieve their goal. This element should be easy to recognize, because it's easy to initiate. It derives from saying or thinking, "I want" or "I need." These gestures constitute a desire, which doubles as a person's passion.

Most people have at least *some* desire to do things that will enhance their life. I say most people, because there are some who are unhappy with their life, yet have no desire to do anything different than what they're doing, or they give up at the moment they encounter an obstacle. This implies that the obstacle's ability to defeat them is stronger than their desire to succeed, which cannot occur while they're trying to improve their life. It's also important to note that desire alone won't completely facilitate the needed changes. A person has to go deeper, as there are three more elements in the formula.

The second letter is O, and it stands for *opportunity*. This is the method in which you'll achieve your goal. This is the de facto catalyst in achieving a goal. If you execute a plan to make the best of an opportunity, your goal may be within reach, but not quite. I have to explain the last two elements, but here's some valuable information on opportunity.

Opportunity can present itself in a variety of ways. Someone may be trying to show you how to do something, sell or give you something. Maybe you've discovered a new device or service. Opportunity is the most difficult element in the DOME formula, because most of the time it comes from an outside entity, while desire is created solely by you.

Many of us have seen a product and wondered, *"How come I couldn't have come up with that idea?"* Don't worry – it's happened to the best of us. The interesting thing about opportunity is it's normally where many people become stuck. I'll explain more on this in a minute.

Once you've found an opportunity, the next step is to form and execute a workable plan to capitalize on it, and tip the scales to your advantage. This sets the stage for the next element in the DOME formula: M.

M is the *means*. The means is when the rubber meets the road. How do you get to the goal? The means is the method of action taken in response to the presented circumstances. It can refer to financial backing, support received, physical ability, or whatever you deem necessary to execute the plan.

I keep saying you need to be prepared for the unexpected. Sometimes, the only means you need is located *between your ears*. Whatever is used to advance an opportunity is the means. Opportunity and means are complimentary. You can't achieve one without the other being presented, first. For the formula to work, an opportunity must be in place before securing the means to pursue the opportunity.

I refer to the means as "the bridge" in the formula, because no matter how strong your desire is, or how great the opportunity may be, if you don't have the means, it *"just ain't gonna happen!"* You need to put action and know-how behind the desire and opportunity in order to get the train moving.

E is of course the final letter in the formula, and it stands for *education*. This is the know-how. I refer to it as "the glue," because it holds everything together. If I had to choose one element as most important, education would be the one. Why? You can have the other three elements in place and reach your goal. However, maintaining that level of success requires education. You don't want to revert to the same mindset and habits that got you into the rut in the first place.

Does this mean you need to spend thousands of dollars on formal education? Not necessarily. Unless your goal requires something to the contrary, you may already possess all the tools you need. With the abundance of information available online, you can learn about any subject by doing research. Use the internet for knowledge *and* entertainment!

To illustrate the importance of education, I direct your attention to the countless celebrities who have come into, and gone out of the limelight. In the following scenario, feel free to insert any celebrity you believe would fit what I describe. Have someone in mind? Maybe… maybe not, but here goes:

The person arrives on the scene and blows up. They're blazing up the trail like wildfire. They're traveling the world, wearing expensive designer clothes, ridiculously oversized jewelry, and living in a huge house with 15 cars in the garage (some they've never driven), to name a few luxuries.

Fast forward a few years, and the same person is barely making ends meet! You read stories about them filing for bankruptcy protection, working menial jobs, or see media illustrations of them on the fast track to destruction. How in the world does this occur?

Again, the key is balance. Situations like the ones mentioned above occur when one (or more) of the elements outweighs the others, creating an *imbalance*. The desire may be stronger than the opportunity. The opportunity may be stronger than the means. The means may be stronger than the education. Imbalance creates issues, increases stress, and produces obstacles. It's one of the causes of self-defeatism.

Your chosen celebrity likely ran into issues because of this imbalance. Using my description of the DOME formula, it should be easier to see how the breakdown occurred. They had a strong desire, were given a golden opportunity, and were able to secure the means to execute a plan. However, the education wasn't equal to the other elements, and their plan collapsed.

Maybe the athlete hired someone to take care of their money without taking time to educate themselves (at least minimally) on the importance of creating residual income and bookkeeping. They let someone else keep track of their finances without knowing how to do the basics themselves. Now… *"Money gone!"*

Maybe the hip-hop artist didn't realize a large property tax bill comes along with that huge house, or didn't realize that *"1 of only 60 made in the world"* sports car was designed so you can't, and probably *shouldn't* take it to the local mechanic for maintenance. Perhaps the singer didn't realize the majority of their income is supposed to come from touring and brand management, not from record sales. Maybe they didn't know taking a large cash advance isn't the wisest thing to do without an effective marketing and promotion strategy.

Any number of things may have been contributing factors, and I'm not implying these people are stupid. However, after reading and hearing some of their stories, I'd be hard-pressed to say a percentage of them weren't being stupid, at some point. It's probably a good thing I'm not mentioning names! I feel confident in saying most of them were perhaps not educated enough to minimize the impact of the disastrous situations they found themselves in.

To the everyday person, these scenarios may seem far-fetched, but what happens to the celebrity can happen to the regular Joe. It may not happen on a grand stage where the world can be witnesses to their downfall, but it happens.

It's less traumatic when a regular person experiences misfortune, because millions of people don't hear about it. It's a big deal for the person going through it however, and it can be devastating. Maybe instead of an accountant stealing their money, their electricity is cut off. Instead of dealing with a stalker, their phone is disconnected. Instead of a paternity suit, they have mounting car repair costs. The circumstances may differ, but the category is the same.

I'm sure a few people have figured out by transposing the letters, another acronym can be formed: MODE. You can use MODE with the same meanings for each of the letters. I chose DOME to identify my formula, because I believe everything you accomplish in life begins with *desire!* You can have all the opportunity, means and education in the world; without a desire for something different, you'll never see anything change.

I've outlined the DOME formula elements. You should also have a pretty clear idea of how important balance is to successfully utilizing them, as well. It's time to put them into practice. According to my way of thinking (which I'm certain you've seen can vastly differ from popular opinion), the best way to put a plan in motion is to visualize the end result, *first.*

What?! Yes, I want you to visualize yourself at your goal, then, work backwards to where you are now. By working backwards, you will see that your success is determined by being educated enough to minimize the missteps. What is it going to take for you to achieve the level of success you desire? Once you reach your goal, how much education will it take to maintain that success? Does the education have to be formal, or can you informally obtain it?

Important note: You don't have to put your goal on hold until you become educated. Education should be ongoing, and never-ending. You're never too old (or young) to learn something. You also can never allow yourself to stop learning! There are things to learn on the journey *to* success, as well as while enjoying that success. Now, watch how incredibly *easy* it is to apply the DOME formula to your life.

If you took the time to visualize yourself achieving your goal, you've just expressed a desire to do something different than what you're currently doing. This is why *desire* is the easiest of the DOME elements. You don't expend anything more than your own brainpower to achieve this portion.

Awesome, but did you notice what *else* happened? I'm not sure whether you caught it or not, so I'll point it out: two of the elements in the formula have been *identified!* Education and desire make up half of the formula. Take a bow, because 50% of your battle has been planned, and 25% of it has been *accomplished!* How freaking easy was that?! Now, let's get to work on the other 50%.

Finding an opportunity can be as painstaking as it is challenging. More people get stuck at this element more than any other. This is because opportunity is where obstacles are likely to appear. Instead of pushing through and overcoming the obstacles, a person may decide to stop pursuing the *goal.* Why? Success is designed to weed out the non-passionate person, and the status quo is the safety net (or comfort zone) many people have conditioned themselves to heavily rely on.

Achieving success takes persistence. Persistence takes patience. Both these things take time, which too many people think they don't have enough of. With all the newly-discovered technological advances, patience has become in short supply. Everything is *"I want it, and I want it right now."* We look for the instant gratification, when the more effective way to accomplish things is to slow down. Success in life is a marathon. It's not a sprint!

We want everything "now." We become frustrated when reality's "now" doesn't match the "now" we've developed in our head. This sounds like the desire is heavier than the other three elements, doesn't it? *Bam...* there's that imbalance influencing the outcome of a task or goal – and it was formed without help from any outside entities!

When you decide to pursue a goal, you're going to encounter obstacles. I've said this several times now. If you're not strong enough to summon the courage to stay on the course, you're doomed to fail every time. You must learn to "reject" rejection. Becoming figuratively hard-headed (in this sense) gives you an opportunity to achieve a lot more.

Now, here's the kicker: most obstacles can be overcome with a shift in your thinking. This is because we tend to be much harder on ourselves than another person can ever be. As a result, we can defeat ourselves faster than another person or task will, and it's normally due to the amount of emotional weight we assign to the obstacle. Shifting your mindset and perception drastically reduces the effects of this.

One of my favorite original philosophies is, *"Failure isn't an option, because I don't make it one."* I refuse to acknowledge failure as a viable option, but it doesn't mean I refuse to acknowledge the *possibility* of failure. It means, once I set a goal, the fear of failing doesn't deter me from striving toward the goal, although it may alter my plan to get it.

I'm not insinuating that I've never failed at anything. I've failed many times, at many things. I've been married twice, so apparently I sucked at being married at least once. Had I allowed failure to be the *"end all, be all"* I wouldn't be married to (at least in *my* eyes), hands down, the most amazing woman on the planet! I don't give failure a chance to defeat me, because I decide when I will stop pursuing a goal.

So, you've found an opportunity you believe will get you to your goal. What's next? Find the means to take advantage of that opportunity. Whatever you need to convert the opportunity into reality, find a way to get it. If you can't *find* an opportunity, *create* one! Never allow yourself to be obstructed from success by self-doubt.

Securing a method to make an opportunity work can be long and drawn out. Applying for a loan or grant, obtaining a patent or copyright, or looking for investors can take a lot of time and effort. Finding someone to back your endeavors without discouragement can be tough, unless you deal with family members or friends. You must still convince them your idea is worth their investment. They're assuming all the risks, while you get the freedom to chase your dreams.

Business and family are touchy subjects that usually don't mix well. I advise anyone against doing it unless you're left with *no* other alternative. Even then, you should *still* think twice! Family can take business arrangements casually *because* they're family. Not a headache you need, or want!

Another reason many people give up at the opportunity stage of the formula is that they get tired of hearing *"no."* How ironic is that? Saying no to other people is okay, but hearing it said to you gets you bent out of shape.

Repeatedly hearing *no* can promote negative perceptions in a person's head. They begin to accept "no" as the norm by falsely thinking, *"That's just the way it's supposed to be."* Be mindful of the damage the word *no* can cause.

This is where it's beneficial to develop a layer of thick skin. You need to be able to push through barriers. Standing still has never made much of an impact on society, other than the invention of the traffic light, and stop signs.

To execute a plan to make an opportunity successful, you'll need to find the person who's willing to go as far out on a limb as you are. Once you find them, and they agree to assist you, you will have your means. At this point, you should be able to see, feel, smell, and taste your goal. All that's left is to obtain, and apply the necessary education.

Education will ensure you effectively apply the means to execute the opportunity successfully. Do this correctly and you won't end up back at square one, making excuses for why it wasn't successful, trying to convince people to present you with opportunity a second time, armed with only a desire.

So, how do I tie all the chapters together, and assist you in creating an improvement plan that works? The odds of being happy and successful are decreased when you develop incorrect perceptions of the circumstances presented to you.

Examining how you see these things is what I've been trying to help you to focus on throughout this book. I've used myself in many of the examples, to show you how easy it is to *create* these barriers using only your mind, but it's just as easy to get started knocking them down.

A step in the right direction is ensuring you understand the importance of balance and self-honesty. You must accept that you can't do everything perfectly, and embrace your shortcomings. This can be difficult if you've just discovered you don't have things as together as you previously thought, but shortcomings are temporary. You become better by facing them head-on! You may have chosen not to face them before, but you now know you can (and will) survive!

Learn how to step away from your comfort zone. I was told while playing Little League baseball, *"You're never going to hit the ball if you don't take the damned bat off your shoulder and swing it!"* Yes, my Little League coach said *damned* to a 10-year old! Guess what? I heard it, endured it, and turned out just fine.

I said earlier, sometimes you have to throw caution to the wind if you want to grow. While you're learning to hit, you're going to miss the ball a lot. That's not enough reason to stop swinging the bat! With coaching, your swing naturally gets better the more you swing the bat. Swing it enough times, and it's only a matter of time before you hit the ball.

You also have to learn to turn a deaf ear and a blind eye to nay-sayers. There will be plenty along the road to success, especially if they have no clue of, or are disinterested in what you're trying to accomplish. It's easy to discourage a person from doing something when you have no desire to do it yourself. You can never allow anyone to convince you that *you* can't achieve *your* goal.

Sometimes, the people closest to you will be the biggest nay-sayers. This is because they believe they can say anything they want and you're supposed to listen to them. Why? You hold their opinion in high regard. The more emotional weight you attach to the person's opinion, the more likely you'll react with that anticipated response. Or maybe they're trying to advance an agenda, and banking on an emotional reaction. You can throw their game off by not providing one.

Be prepared for, and able to accept criticism and scrutiny. If you can't take these in stride while continuing to push toward your goal, you're *not* ready to take on success. As you become successful, you'll have to deal with unchartered levels of criticism, and it isn't always constructive. If you can't do what's right *for* you despite what's being said *about* you, criticism is going to pick you apart, and it won't take long for it to pick up steam and become as ruthless as peer pressure.

You must learn to get (and stay) out of your own way. Intentionally engaging in self-destructive behavior makes your life stagnate. You have to keep moving. Remaining immobile keeps you staring at your goal from a distance, and the distance won't get any shorter by you *looking* at it! The view isn't going to change... until *you* do!

Make it a practice to keep emotions as far away from your decision-making as possible. You've read how emotions can affect a situation. Knee-jerk reactions are rarely effective, and if they're wrong (as many times, they *are*), you must go back and say, *"My bad."* They only trigger rushed, panicked decisions, and when you're panicked, you'll make decisions you normally wouldn't make. Panic serves to promote chaos, and who wants to deal with *that* on a regular basis?

Stop unnecessarily stressing yourself by taking on more than you should, dealing with extremes, or by reacting prematurely, or over-emotionally. You will instantly shift an atmosphere's tone, and it may not be for the better! This also goes for internalizing situations, and making them personal. You'll react differently, and *emotions should never override reason!*

Trust the people on your team and stop judging their performance by your standards. They're *not you!* They may not use the methods you use, or do the things you do. Do minor variances in the method of doing really matter, if the task is getting done sufficiently? Loosen up! It will alleviate a lot of stress, and you won't have as many issues to "fix." You will become more productive by adopting this methodology.

Find a mentor who can provide support and guidance. Contrary to popular belief, mentors aren't just for young people. Every person you talk to has taken a unique path to get to where they are. However, *any* person you talk to may be holding the information you need to get you where you want to be. You're never going to find it, if you embrace solitude. You must interact with as many people as you can.

Next, you must forgive the people who've done you wrong. This sounds *crazy*, and I'm not saying do it for *them*. Do it for *you!* People may have done terrible things *to* you, or said terrible things *about* you. You must forgive them… for your sanity's sake. You can't forget what they did or said, and I'm in no way saying you should, but keeping it in the front of your mind keeps you preoccupied with anger, resentment, and revenge, and it's stunting your emotional growth.

While we're on the subject of forgiveness, if the person is trying to make amends for, or correct behavior they exhibited in the past, regardless of what *you think* their motive is for doing so, do yourself a favor and give them the benefit of the doubt. I said a person can't escape their personality, but I also said they can always change their tactics. What *also* needs to change is your perception of their behavior. The latter doesn't always happen. Why not?

It's because you become fixated on the behavior, and regularly get upset about it, due to the amount of emotional weight you assign. You end up getting "stuck," and hold the grudge for as long as you choose to hold it.

Is it reasonable to force a person to *eternally* pay for behavior or actions that occurred in the past, but haven't occurred since? Possibly, but here's something you may not have considered: Who's *really* paying the price?

The person may have matured, truly be trying to move passed an incident, or has gotten over it, but you are *insistent* on making them (*and you*) relive it! They get *no* slack from you. Would you like to know why? It's because you feel empowered that you can finally show, or tell them how their actions affected you. You're finally "in control," and you're going to let them know, every chance you get!

I'll point this out again: the issue is more about *your satisfaction*, and not so much about their behavior, or action. Could one of those core principles be being devalued by *you?*

I said this in Chapter 7 and I'll reiterate it: you must, must, *must* stop dredging up things from the past (or present), if the *only* thing they do is make you mad. You already know how these things affect you, because you're constantly rehashing them. Figuratively speaking, you're stuck. How? You're doing what I *also* alluded to in Chapter 7 – *holding the future hostage, with present actions based on past experience.*

The people or things that hurt you are clueless to how you were truly affected. You couldn't control the event back then, and certainly can't undo what's already been done. Why not do the best thing for you, and alter your reaction to it? If you can learn to let go of the anger, life will take care of itself. Holding onto grudges is only holding *you* back!

Finally, I highly encourage you to consider applying the DOME formula to your life. I'm telling you, it works! There are only four elements to it, but balancing them efficiently can mean the difference between achieving, and not achieving a goal you've set. I've battle-tested it many times and I'm happy to say, it has held up in every scenario thus far.

| D – Desire | O – Opportunity |
| M – Means | E – Education |

DOME formula elements

If you take nothing *else* away from this book, accept the DOME formula as my gift. Apply it to as many aspects of your life as you need to. I'm living the proof that inspiration can literally come from anywhere, and you can reach any goal, if you're willing to do what's necessary to achieve it.

I've endured intense scrutiny for telling other people my goals. Sometimes, I think about those who've tried to discourage me. I've concluded that many of them did so because they put their *own* goals on the back burner. I've been laughed and scoffed at, ridiculed, and told I couldn't do what I said I wanted to do. Had I accepted the things nay-sayers said, I wouldn't have accomplished a fraction of the things I've accomplished. I'd be just another person who's remained trapped – afraid to step outside of their comfort zone.

Thankfully, I was exposed to alternative methods and didn't allow negativity to distract me (for long). I figured out what I wanted and summoned the courage to go after it. I learned to keep my goals to myself, and that life will unfold all by itself, if you let it. Becoming an author wasn't the path I envisioned for myself in Oakland. Destiny had its own plans.

Despite the adversity I've faced, I've been fortunate enough to be put in a position where I can put my ideas in a written format. This, no doubt subjects me to a variety of opinions. Some people will enjoy what I've written. Others, not so much! That's the price paid for publishing a book.

Whether you found this book useful, or use*less* – agreed, or disagreed with any of the information or opinions I've written, I sincerely appreciate you giving me the opportunity to occupy your mind for a while. It has been an honor to share my thoughts and experiences with you. The beauty of our society is we don't always have to agree. We can disagree without being disagreeable. I stated at the beginning of this book, I didn't have the solution to every problem; at the end of the book... I *still* don't.

The bottom line is whatever changes you find necessary to facilitate a more enjoyable life for yourself, step up to the challenge and make them happen! Don't *"think about it..."* just *do* it! Some people need religion to help them. Others need a pet, a vacation, to quit drinking, or smoking (cigarettes and/or other things), meditation, to distance themselves from toxic people, or to go to the gym. Perhaps they need human companionship in their life. Of course, if you believe human companionship is what's missing, make sure not only that you've read, but have a full understanding of Chapter 7.

Greatness is lurking inside of you. It's up to you, to summon the courage to tap into your abilities, and bring it to the surface. Society is in desperate need of it. If your previously chosen direction has only resulted in you running into walls, with nothing to show for your efforts except battle scars, a simple shift in direction may be what's necessary. Keep Mr. Einstein's definition of insanity in mind.

Acting on the desire to change an aspect of your life is one of the most frightening decisions you'll ever *have* to make, because of what you may find is required of you to facilitate the change. However, it is one of the bravest decisions you *can* make. You can't be afraid to be you, regardless of what someone else says about, or thinks of you, or your decisions.

The journey to improvement, success, and happiness, just like any other, must begin with a desire. I know many of the things I suggested in this book are easier said than done, but they can be done. I know, because I've done them!

Improving your life may not be easy, but the reward is worth the risk. The journey is grueling and at times, extremely frustrating. With achieving goals, it's simple: you'll either find a way to achieve it, or find a way to justify why you haven't! Which of these two can you live with? Famed motivational speaker Les Brown said, *"Most people fail in life not because they aim too high and miss, but because they aim too low and hit."*

At the beginning of your turnaround, you'll be staring at a tall task, but a task easily accomplished by shifting your thinking. An understanding of "why" reduces, or may even eliminate the figurative "gamble" needed to improve your life. The key is being willing and confident enough to initiate the shift, despite the obstacles or fears that may, or may *not* be in your way. You're stronger and more resilient than you realize.

The difference between now and when you began this book, is now you have a few more methods you can use to help you start shifting the odds into your favor. Clearing out the *"emotional clutter"* can be intimidating, but all it takes is the first step: act on the desire, and make the decision to start the cleanup. Then, start tackling the obstacles the same way they were introduced… one at a time. My hope is something I've written makes the obstacles and that tall task *less* intimidating.

I sincerely wish you the best of luck with transforming your life. I've given you enough information to get you a seat at the table. The amount you're willing to *wager*, and the way you play your *hand*… is completely up to *you!*

Bibliography

(2016). Retrieved from NBA Encyclopedia - Playoff Edition: http://www.nba.com/history/players/jordan_stats.html

Meyer, P. J. (2003). *Attitude Is Everything: If You Want to Succeed Above and Beyond.* Waco, TX: Meyer Resource Group.

PBS. (1995). *The Long Walk of Nelson Mandela - Chronology Timeline.* Retrieved from PBS Frontline: http://www.pbs.org/wgbh/pages/frontline/shows/mandela/etc/cron.html

Williamson, M. (1992). *A Return to Love: Reflections on the Principles of a Course in Miracles.* New York, NY: HarperCollins.

About the Author

Oakland, California native Kevin E. Eastman thrives on simplicity and logic. A skilled speaker, mentor, and community activist with a *"tell it like it is"* mentality, he shoots straight from the hip when it comes to assisting people with their personal development. A graduate of Castlemont High School, he served over 20 years on active duty in the United States Air Force, in multiple capacities at locations around the world.

A number of his professional positions have involved mentoring. He began by teaching basic Air Force doctrine to new recruits as a Military Training Instructor, commonly known as a Drill Instructor. He continued by interacting with thousands of people, in over a decade as a recruiter. These positions helped him develop his passion for assisting people with achieving their goals.

Kevin has earned academic degrees from the Community College of the Air Force, Columbia Southern University, and Azusa Pacific University. He is certified in Marketing, Professional Selling Skills, and Sales Coaching. Married with two daughters, he enjoys being involved with community improvement and development efforts as a member of Alpha Phi Alpha Fraternity, Inc., sports, traveling, listening to music, writing, reading, cooking, and spending time with family and friends.

Kevin enjoys interacting with readers. Share your experiences, successes, comments, and feedback. Visit www.kevineeastman.com.
You can also keep in contact through social media:
Facebook: @authorkevineeastman
Twitter: @eastke1
Instagram: @eastke1